# Broken Spirit, Stolen Innocence

## By
## Marwen

PublishAmerica
Baltimore

First printing.

ISBN: 1-4137-7001-0
PUBLISHED BY PUBLISHAMERICA, LLLP
www.publishamerica.com
Baltimore

Printed in the United States of America

# Dedication

This book is dedicated to the Holy Trinity: Father, Son and the Holy Spirit; Mama Maria; and St. Therese.

I will always be thankful to whomever it was that was asking for the intercession of St. Therese and praying to get me back on my feet, into the Church, and for my return to God.

I thank God for the creation of this book, and the Holy Spirit for the inspiration, as I have never written anything before and had no idea that I could even do it!

I thank Father John Paul Villanueva for his constant help and encouragement.

My friend, Betty, gave me the idea that I should write my story. Here is the result, so she is definitely included in the dedication.

I also thank my children, Bernie, Brenda and Marcel, for never discouraging me or saying that it was a crazy and weird idea, and for helping me whenever necessary.

I thank my publishers for having faith in me and my abilities!

May God bless them all!

# Introduction

This is a very true account of what can happen if you are too innocent and gullible and believe other people whether you should or not. Believe me, most of the time you should not listen to them. As soon as somebody tells you it is only for your own good, beware, because most of the time it is *not for your good but for theirs*!

This is a very painful experience to write all this down, because it brings back things I don't want to remember anymore. The danger of falling into Satan's hands again is also there, but I have done this so you will realize the danger is there, and contrary to what people want to believe, the devil can get at you in a way you would not ever have believed possible! Don't ever think that you are a cut above doing something like this. I fell into it and, believe it or not, *SO CAN YOU!*

I am writing this with the help of the Holy Spirit, who wants to have this published to help others stay out of the devil's hands. I am still struggling and know that without God's help I wouldn't be doing this, neither would I be where I am at now and feeling free as a bird again after years of what I now consider and know it to have been torture, slow and painful.

I am still not quite the same person I was before all this started, neither will I ever be that way again, because my spirit has been broken and my innocence has been stolen from me. That will never come back again!

I have more of the sense of sinfulness then a lot of other people. The innocence, what you have without the devil on your heels and inside of you, the natural innocence that most people have and that you have been born with, has been shattered and will never come back again. It is almost like losing your virginity. Once it is gone, it cannot be brought back.

But I have peace of mind and feel secure in the knowledge that God is with me and the Holy Spirit is looking after me. My guardian angel is with me, and I only have to call on the Holy Trinity and Jesus will be there for me with Mama Maria close behind Him!

Why did I ever think I needed anything else in my life but the infinite love and compassion of God? Nobody needs anything or anyone else!

*Jesus, I love You!*
*Mama Maria, I love You!*

# Chapter 1
# Trials and Tribulations

I will start in February of 1995, when the owner of the apartment building where I was the building manager decided he would rather have a superintendent couple in the building than a building manager with a cleaning and a maintenance staff. So, I was out of a job, with no money coming in and no backup whatsoever!

I was told I had to move out, but I held on to my apartment. The tenants were backing me up, and I even typed up a letter that they all signed. The tenets even held back their rent cheques for two months out of solidarity, because for one or another reason they felt safe as long as I was in the building.

May be it was all the soup and sandwiches I made for them when they were sick. A lot of them were seniors, and they all knew I could do some mean cooking, so when they needed help or could smell I was cooking, they knew who to go to and how to get me to give them some food.

They did not want me to leave, which gave me a good feeling. It didn't help any as far as money was concerned, but it made me feel good!

Since I am divorced and without any alimony, I was in a bad situation. I stuck it out in the building, said novenas, prayed to God to please, please, please help me out of my predicament, but nothing happened.

On April 27 I sat in my kitchen, made myself a drink and sat down, utterly devastated, without any hope and nothing to do. I saw myself as bag lady on the street and, of course, that started the tears flowing but good.

And then I couldn't move my arm or hand, the drink was as if glued to my hand, and I thought that they were trying to poison me. I punched in number 1 on the phone, which went automatically through to my daughter's place. She lived very close by, and I told her that I couldn't move and that "they," whoever that were, were trying to poison me.

Well, Mike and Brenda showed up in no time, and Mike came over and gently took the drink from my hand and drank it to show me that there was nothing the matter with the drink and that it was all in my head, which was true!

We started talking and decided that we should phone Dale, a friend of my oldest son, who lived in the building and he came over and between the four of us we decided that I needed a psychiatrist. So they finally left at about ten o'clock and I went to bed after begging God to please help me.

# Chapter 2
# God's Divine Intervention

Well, the next morning after I got up and had coffee, about 10:30 a.m., I decided to check my Lottery 6/49 tickets, which I had literally bought with my last money. I marked off six numbers! Can you believe it?

I just sat there quietly looking at them and thought, I won! I won! If I have five numbers on the next row, I know for sure I'm not dreaming!"

And sure enough, I had five numbers on the next row, which meant I had won the first and the second prize. Just to make sure, I took the ticket to Suzie at the convenience store. She was so excited and told me I had won a little over a million dollars, because there was another winner somewhere else! Can you imagine how I felt?

I went home and thanked God on my knees for listening to my prayers, because the night before I had said, "Lord, I have said novenas, I have prayed, begged and prayed some more for help. I have spent my last money and will have nothing left. I will be a baglady!"

And all the while God had listened to me and did His own thing in his own time!

Of course the first one I phoned was Brenda at work and told her that I had found my psychiatrist.

She said, "Oh, Mom, what is his name? Is his office downtown? I'll take time off and go with you."

I told her, "Yes, his name is the Lotto 6/49, and yes, it is downtown, and yes, I want you to go with me."

So she answered me, "I don't know what you're talking about, but I'll take the day off and be there as soon as I can. Now you just relax. We will sort it all out when I get there."

Of course she didn't believe me after the scene from the night before. She thought I had really lost it this time! She went to her boss, who knew us and knew about the whole situation, and said, "I don't know what is going on, but my mom thinks she has won the lottery, so I would like to go home and find out what is going on."

She got the day off, came in my apartment, hugged and kissed me and said, "Okay, where are the tickets!"

I showed them to her and, of course, there were more tears and hugs. But this time the tears were from sheer happiness, I can tell you that!

In the meantime that Brenda was on her way to me I had phoned Joe, a friend of ours who is a financial planner, and told him the happy news. I asked him if he wanted to take care of my finances. He asked his boss, who told him that for a million dollar account you don't stay in the office, you just go and get it! So Joe met us at the lottery office.

# Chapter 3
# The Celebration

You can imagine that the whole world seemed rosy and incredibly good, and I was happy as a lark, naturally! I had phoned Marcel, my youngest son, and tried to phone my oldest son, Bernie, but I could not get hold of him. Marcel picked up his wife, and we all met at the lotto office downtown.

On our way to the lottery office, Brenda very cautiously mentioned that she did not want to intrude on private domain, but wondered whether I had given any thought to investments. I told her I was way ahead of her, and Joe was meeting us at the lottery office! By the time we got there, Marcel, Judy and Joe were there already. The money was sent directly to Joe's office and bank to start right away making money for me! Joe has always been terrific, and I couldn't have had a better adviser! I know I have given him a rough time sometimes, but that was part and parcel of the trouble I was in.

At the lotto office they asked me if I wanted to publicize my winnings and I said yes, because the tenants in the building had supported me so much that it would not have been fair to them if I did not let them know what had happened.

I had an interview with somebody at the lotto office, who asked me where I had bought the tickets. I couldn't remember it right away and so I said I had gotten them at Suzie's convenience store. Then I said, "Oh no! I actually bought them in the hospital."

Well, then I had to tell them the whole story of how I bought them at the hospital. I told them it was because I gave somebody a ride who couldn't drive anymore because he was on oxygen. I had also helped him with his veteran's pension. Something had gone wrong, and it had to be straightened out. Since he had no nearby relatives to help him, I did the job.

Boy, did they ever make a sob story out of that one! The reward you get when you do something good for someone! I couldn't believe it when I heard that one.

When we got out of the lottery office the staff told the people that I was the big winner, so people were looking at us. Since everyone who was there had won something or other, they were all happy and smiling, so everyone shouted congratulations and good luck and so on. I tell you, it is quite the trip!

Then we did some shopping, bought some liquor, cold drinks, food, ordered pizzas, and then everyone took the day off and we went to my place and started to celebrate in earnest.

At six o'clock that evening the news was spread on TV, and the tenants came marching to my place, congratulating me and telling me it couldn't have happened to a better person and that I deserved it. It was pandemonium, I tell you!

Everyone came in, had a drink and walked around. Everyone was talking to everyone else, and all I did was nod and laugh and tell the story over and over.

I think at one point Brenda felt sorry for me, so she started telling the story, but the people wanted to hear it from me. You know how that goes, they wanted to hear it from the horse's mouth so to speak!

And finally I got a hold of Bernie, my oldest son, who had been working out of town. He finally arrived when all had left at 1:30 in the morning, so we had a good laugh and a couple of drinks, and then I finally went to sleep at 5 o'clock in the morning!

# Chapter 4
# Thank You, God!

The next morning I went to church and thanked God for my good fortune and put an ad in the newspaper to thank St. Jude for his intervention. I have three brothers and sisters. Two brothers and two sisters live in Holland, one brother lives in Los Angeles, and one sister lives in San Francisco, California. Of course I phoned them all, and they were as happy as I was. They considered, since they all had money, that it was nice of me to join the club!

Since my apartment had been previously broken into, I have always been sure that the owner had the handyman do this job for him. I did not feel safe in that place anymore, so I took with me what I wanted and gave the rest away to a girl I knew who had little stuff of her own. It made her happy, and it did the same for me!

I phoned a friend who was the security director at the Royal York and asked him for a nice suite. He told me to come on down and he would personally see to it that I was taken care of!

Well, that was another trip! I was royally installed in a suite with a separate living room and bedroom, a fantastic bathroom, and a bottle of wine and fruit was waiting for me. Oh man, I felt like a queen! I stayed there for a few days, and I had a great time just wandering around and looking at the stores with the knowledge that if I wanted to, I could buy the things!

I bought my first outfit in the Royal York, and even now I still get comments on it. You get what you pay for! We had a dinner with my children and some friends in the Japanese restaurant there and were treated like royalty. I was introduced to the owner, who looked personally after us, and everyone was staring at us to see who the "royalty" was who got this kind of treatment! It was great!

I had a little old car, a Tempo, and the children had told me that the thing was not safe to drive anymore and to get a new car right away. Well, I was about ready to buy a new car, and Brenda had taken the rest of the week off, so we went shopping for a car in earnest. We went shopping around downtown, and I tried a few cars out, but I didn't really like any of the cars we tried out.

I could not make up my mind what I wanted except that I knew what I wanted but just had not found it yet.

We tried a couple of them out, but I really didn't like any of them, so we went home with a lot of information on cars, but disappointed because I couldn't find what I wanted.

On Saturday morning, Brenda and her friend Mike and I went shopping again. When we passed City Buick I thought it would be a good idea if we went there to look around. Well, in the front was nothing I liked, and I definitely wanted a white or light coloured car. So we drove to the back and there I saw MY CAR! It was a beautiful pearl coloured Cadillac Eldorado! I told them that was my car!

A salesman came over, introduced himself and asked if he could help us. I told him yes and showed him my car. He told me that was fine, that he would order me one, to which I replied that he didn't get the picture. THIS one was MY CAR, and no other one would do. He replied that this particular one was the first one of its kind in Toronto, and it was not even put on the computer yet because it had just come off the truck. I said that that was fine with me and asked whether he wanted a sale or not!

He checked with the manager and, sure enough, the car was mine!

Since this was the first big purchase I had made, it was quite a trip to tell him that, yes, I wanted to pay cash for the car, was that all right? He jokingly said that I must have won the lottery, and I said, yes, that is exactly what happened. We had a good laugh over that, but he talked to Joe and all was okay after that! It is amazing how things change for you when you have money behind you!

And when I picked up my car after two days it was such a dream come true. People even honked their horns, rolled their windows down at the stoplights and shouted, "What a car!" It was indeed the first one in Toronto with the V32 motor and, oh man, was I proud of that car! It was a two-door and looked like a sports car with an open roof top and everything in it and under it and over it!

I did some shopping on my own too. After all, it was nice to be able to buy clothes without having to look at the price and to be able to actually buy clothes that were still in style as opposed to only being able to buy them when they were cheaper. By then they were actually already out of style, but you couldn't afford them before at the high price when they were still in season.

And after that it was high-time for a good holiday. I hadn't had a holiday in about fourteen years! I asked all of my kids if they wanted to go on a holiday, but none had the time except Brenda, who only had one week holidays, so I booked a flight to Aruba and off we went!

We went first class, and that in itself is an experience. You get a nice glass of wine after you sit down, and you get so pampered. We had a drink before dinner—and that dinner was really something else! There is actually a menu that you can choose from when you fly first class, with coffee and liqueur after.

We had a marvelous flight and soon arrived in Aruba, where we were the first ones to embark and get the royal treatment. You eventually get used to it. There could have been confusion to get the luggage, but since everything was arranged by my travel agency, there was no confusion. It went so smooth and carefree because you can leave it to the porters, who will get you through customs and all that stuff in no time, and that is what we did.

We were picked up at the airport and were driven to the Tamaryn, where we were staying. It was quite the experience, I can tell you that! We had a marvelous time in Aruba. It was my first encounter with the Caribbean islands, and I loved it! I think it is such a beautiful island, the people are so laid-back and easygoing. I still was not used to that because for years I had literally slaved for this guy, working up to 16 or 18 hours a day, and I didn't know how to relax anymore! I had a hard time getting used to the idea that I did not have to run around anymore and that I really could relax!

The doorman at the Tamaryn, James, told me to relax, that the place would still be there the next day. He said I should have a drink, soak up the sun, make some friends, go for a swim, go for a walk…he said I was there to do nothing and they were there to make it happen for me!

We went shopping and bought clothes and bathing suits and had a marvelous time picking out things for the ones left behind in Toronto. We went to explore the island. It was just one fun-filled week, which we deserved after all the hassle I had been through!

After we got back we had the pleasure of handing out the stuff we had accumulated for the ones left behind in Toronto, so the homecoming was as nice as the take off.

# Chapter 5
# A Place to Live

I also had to find a place to live, and I found a condominium that I liked. I had what I thought was a beautiful penthouse condominium, so I filled out all the papers, signed them and thought I was all set. I got a phone call the next day that the condominium I had rented was double-booked, and they offered me another one at a different spot.

Thinking back on all that has happened since then, everything seemed to come to the climax of getting me in the spot where I ended up!

Of course I told them that it really didn't matter to me where I went as long as it was not a dump, and the real estate girl took me to another condominium building, which I thought was even better than the other one. It had so many extras, the facilities were enormous, there were two swimming pools (the inside one had a sauna with two whirlpools, and the outside one had a barbecue area with five barbecues that you could reserve), two tennis courts and a walking area. It was beautiful, with lots of flowers, trees and plants, and it looked great.

Inside there was a big gym with all sorts of equipment with an open area for yoga classes and such. Than there was a room with pool tables, a table tennis room, two libraries, two card rooms, a party room for 150 people with a kitchen and a bar. There was a big television screen for movies and there was even a bowling room!

Well, after all that I filled out the papers that were necessary in a hurry, and this time everything really was all right! Since I wasn't sure if I wanted to live in this particular area, because I had lived in the Beaches before, I rented the place for two years and thought I could always see what I wanted to do after that.

Since I then had an idea what kind of space I was getting, it was time to go for some serious shopping for furniture with my daughter. We went to Leon's with a friend of hers who was getting married and also wanted to look at furniture. Just like in any other store you go to, the first thing we had was a salesman down our necks, asking if he could help us.

I just wanted to look around, but he kept on hovering over my shoulder, so I looked at Brenda (we are very tuned into one another), who asked him for his name and told him that as soon as I had made up my mind we would call him.

I started to look at the furniture, and the first living room set I saw I really liked. Brenda pointed out that there were so many more to look at and wanted me to at least look at the others too, but I liked what I saw. We wandered around, looked at all the other ones, and Brenda finally agreed with me that I had picked the best one out to start off with. I picked up all the stuff for my new condominium.

I literally bought everything there from the living room to the two bedrooms, the solarium, the kitchen and the dining room! It is such an incredible feeling when you can just shop around and pick up the stuff that you like without having to worry if you can afford it! It is quite a trip, I can tell you!

After picking out what I wanted, we called the salesman over so he could start to write things up. He wrote and wrote, and we were walking around, pointing all the stuff out. I bought a dining room set with a beautiful cupboard, six chairs and two captain chairs. Everything I had picked out was in bleached oak. There were two corner cupboards, an extra cupboard, a living room set with coffee tables and two side tables, a footstool, a bunch of beautiful lamps, two more cupboards for the solarium, and a desk with two small sets of drawers for papers. There was a kitchen set with two chairs, a total bedroom set with dressers, mirrors, side tables and the whole bit. Well, I tell you, his hand started to shake, and he told me he could not believe his good fortune by the size of the order!

By this time the other salesmen were watching what was going on and were kicking their behinds, because we were very casually dressed in shorts and T-shirts, and they didn't think it was worth their while to spend time on us! We finally came to the end of my list, but I still did not have a television or a sound system. Since this was in another department, he asked if it was okay with me if he could call a friend of his over to help me with these items.

We went over there, and by this time the whole store staff was watching us. The salesman told me that I had made not his day, not his week, but his whole month as far as the commission went! After the order was all written up, all three pages of it, he had to get the okay from the management office. I thought I might as well take advantage of the postponement of payment for a year and let that money make more money for me rather than for the owners at Leon's!

But that had to be authorized by the manager, who was one of the owners of the store, and he came over and said jokingly that I must have won the lottery. I tried to get around not answering him and said something like, "Oh sure, that's what everybody thinks!" But then Brenda and Patti, who had been wandering around, came back and he said it again, I looked at Brenda and we both burst out laughing. I finally told him that, yes, I *had* won the lottery.

He wanted to call the whole staff over to give them a lesson in never again discarding people no matter how they were dressed, because you never knew who you had in front of you! Since I didn't feel like being put on the spot and in the limelight, I told the owner as far as I was concerned he could have a conference about this after I had left the store!

And that is what he did. After I had left, I heard it from our salesman later, who after that regarded me as his customer and friend. My wish was his command. From that I actually learned how important it is to dress well. You are regarded by the clothes you wear, and it is important to make sure you look okay. But it was so much fun!

I went to a travel agency and booked a trip to Holland for June. I felt so enormously privileged, and I went on thanking God for my more than good fortune! I went to church on Sundays and went out for breakfast after that, thinking nothing of the fact that I was making people work on the Lord's Day. With that I thought myself to be a good Catholic!

It is amazing how your values change when you get a good kick in the rear end! Now I don't go shopping anymore on Sundays, and if I can avoid it I will not go to a restaurant on Sundays either! It is the Lord's Day, and I spend it mostly in church in the mornings and in prayer; I say the Rosary and Scriptures in the afternoon, and I try to cook ahead of time so I don't have to do any work at dinnertime! I am not saying this to make myself look good, it is just that the difference from before and after are so much in contrast that it is worth mentioning. I still have trouble getting used to the "new" me!

# Chapter 6
# The Start of it All

I had to set up a bank account, and via my financial adviser I was directed to a branch he thought I should deal with, because it was the closest to the new condo I had picked out. He said it was a very good branch and that he had talked to the manager, who was a nice man.

The next day I walked into this branch, but the first day I went there the manager was not in. I sort of got treated shabbily by the girls there, who were more interested in looking at wedding pictures than talking to a stranger. It was the manager's day off, and they didn't even look at me anymore after telling me that he was not in.

I phoned Joe and told him that as far as I was concerned the branch he had sent me to was for the birds, and then I went home. However, I got an apologetic phone call from Joe later on, and he had set up an appointment with the manager for the next day.

I went back there the next day and met the manager, who was very good-looking, charismatic, tall and exactly what I like in a man. I thought, What a guy, he is probably married! I fell for him hook, line and sinker, right then and there. Of course this was the whole of the idea, and as far as I could gather from his reaction, it was the same thing on his side!

To give him a name, we shall call him Tom. That is another thing the devil does, I am pretty sure, that originally he *did* fall for me as much as I fell for him, except in his case it passed by after a while. But for me the devil had taken over, and he was out of the picture except for the fact that the devil was using him to get at me!

To get back to the original story, he apologized all over the place and told his assistant manager to come in and have a good look at me and treat me with respect whenever I came in the branch. As a matter of fact, when we came back from lunch the bank was closed, and he got the whole staff together and asked each one what had happened! I tell you, I felt embarrassed, but after that episode we got down to the nitty-gritty of opening an account.

He asked me how it felt to be a millionaire, and I answered him that it felt great. I had to tell him the story, of course, and in the meantime we were sizing each other up!

When I walked out of the mall that day I saw Tom walking out of the bank at the same time as I was walking by, so we went out together, laughing and joking, I showed him my car since I had just picked up my Cadillac. I was quite proud of that! We talked a bit more, and then I went home.

# Chapter 7
# The Continuance

The day after that he took me out for lunch again, and we talked and talked. By that time I didn't even want to find out anymore whether he was married or not! I think the devil had already got his hooks in me, and I didn't think Tom being married would pose a problem!

I walked out of the bank totally on cloud nine. After setting up my account I went shopping in the mall and pretty well stayed around there the whole day.

But when my daughter met him when she came shopping with me one time, she told me that he was a creep and he gave her the shivers on her back. She couldn't stand him! I couldn't understand her attitude, because I thought he was so terrific. I had so totally fallen for him!

I started to spend most of my days in the mall and started to spend more money than I could afford. I didn't see it that way, of course, because my thinking was already so infiltrated by the devil. I just took all these things for granted! I was walking around the mall every day, all day long, being around Tom all the time, and I didn't even have an inkling or the energy to try to do anything else. I didn't even feel embarrassed doing this; it was just something I did without even realizing what was happening to me!

I did this for a couple of days then, after this, in the middle of the night I woke up with this feeling that someone was trying to get through to me. At first I could not understand who it was, but the sexual feeling I had was so pronounced that it was literally driving me up the wall!

I mentioned a couple of names, but they did nothing. This feeling persisted, but was not acknowledged till I spoke Tom's name. Then the feeling was overwhelming, so incredible sexy, beautiful and totally encompassing. It felt like I was in an enormous embrace, engulfed with such a sexual, sensual overtone that I just gave in and let it wash over me and possess me. I just couldn't resist this loving feeling that seemed to be inside of me and was surrounding me at the same time. I actually could feel Tom's arms around me, holding me in his arms. That was what it felt like!

By that time I knew that Tom was married, and I really didn't want to get involved with a married man, but when I mentioned his name I was a goner for good!

That is when I fell so deeply in love with him that I could not hold back anymore. That was, of course, exactly what the general idea was behind the whole charade! I still had no idea what I had become involved with. I just let it happen to me the way it came, and it seemed an incredible thing!

I couldn't get enough of this, and even during the night I started to tease Tom and say things like, "If you want this or that, make it happen!" The first time he just tossed me over on my stomach and that was that. It was a very effective power play, I can tell you. It showed me exactly who was in charge and not to try him too far, that he could make anything happen. It was very convincing, because after that I didn't even bother to try things like that any more since it would happen the way he wanted it anyway!

I got to be more and more docile and just let things happen. The bad part about this was that I really thought and thoroughly believed that this was exactly what I wanted and was perfectly content with it!

But what I didn't realize was that there was a full moon at the time, because the moon cycles were not something I was into at all. It was the farthest thing from my mind.

But after this I was very, very gradually made to be very aware of the moon. It was done very slowly and over a long period of time, so I didn't really notice it much. It happened so gradually that it was a part of me before I realized what had happened. By that time I was right in the middle of it and took everything for granted!

So each time I was being more and more drawn into this and told that the moon was very important and had special powers. I was told that I had to pay homage to the moon goddess and to be very respectful of what was going on at these times. But like all the other things that were happening, I took everything for granted. My mind was always put at ease about all the things that were happening, so when I started to get messages during the night around either 12 o'clock or around 3 a.m., which is the devil's hour, I was so used to all the things that were already happening that I never thought anything of it. Of course I had no idea of the devil's hour; I didn't even know such a thing existed! And the devil made sure that I never got to know this either!

At first it was only the lovemaking, and then slowly but surely I was told to be quiet for a bit and just relax. I was made to blank my mind so my mind could get a "rest." I was told that it would improve my health when I relaxed my mind.

So of course I had no choice other than to go along with it since I was already so controlled that I wouldn't even have dreamt of going against his wishes.

Then slowly but surely other messages were coming through. Of course, they always came during the night. Things like, "Lie perfectly still, I have to do something now, just lie still, blank your mind, stretch your arms out, you will relax more when they are out of the way. Hold them there, because I have something to do with you that will improve things and will make you more of a part of me." Since I always thought that it was Tom doing these things, I let them happen!

A little while later I had another session, and I was told to stretch my arms out and bend them half up as a sign of surrender. That surrender was total, I can tell you that. I was told to totally surrender to Tom because he knew what was best for me, and I totally surrendered to him!

And the surrender was accompanied by such a beautiful feeling that it couldn't happen enough times as far as I was concerned! That is another way to get you to let him do just what he wants with you! Without realizing what was happening to me, I was totally in the devil's hands and was his toy to do with as he pleased.

The next day I was having lunch with Tom, and he was as happy as I was and started to tell me anecdotes and funny stories. We had a good time and the rest was never mentioned. I thought that this was the way our affair would be worked out, and I was fully prepared to go along with the whole thing!

I will not go into details about this, but I have never had such a sex life in all of my life, and I was married for 19 years before my divorce! At first I thought and said out loud, "This is not for real. This can't be happening to me!" I walked away from the bedroom into my living room and looked out the windows for a few minutes.

When I went back to bed the most incredible, beautiful, sensual and sexual feeling came over me, and it started all over again! That is when I just gave in and experienced the whole thing as beautiful and something I had to get used to! From then on that feeling stayed with me, night and day.

I think this was done because I went on so many cruises and holidays so I would know who was in charge and not try anything on my own!

But by that time I was already so brainwashed that I wouldn't have done anything on my own, even if I would have had the opportunity. I don't think it would have ever entered my mind to try anything that was against the rules!

I was also taken to another mall where they were selling books. I was taken to exactly the place and the book I was supposed to buy and read. Often I was taken somewhere where there was something I was supposed to get, and I would be made to buy it and thought nothing of it. I would just do it!

In the meantime, time was flying by! After the first year in my condominium I noticed that they were erecting a new building in front of me, so I would lose my beautiful view with the most gorgeous sunsets and sunrises! I asked at the office what they were going to build there and when they told me it was going to be another condominium building, I thought it would be a good idea to buy this time!

I talked it over with Tom, and he told me that there was obviously no more room for another building in front of that one, so why not buy a unit in the new building. It only made sense. He told me that he had been in the building and had a look at the units and thought they were better laid out than the one I was in now.

I looked at the plans and thought that either the southwest corner or the northwest corner were the nicest ones, but I looked at the southeast corner and saw all the empty parking lots there and thought it would be better to go the route of the northwest corner. There the only view would be Highway 401 and the industrial area to the north side, which was fine with me. There would be no factories with big smoking pipes or anything like that, just low ground buildings and a plaza with Loblaws. It looked pretty harmless to me, and I decided to buy there.

I had bought the condominium on the condition that I didn't have to take possession till the half of May, since then my rental agreement was up then, and I could move at the end of May. It was a lot of fun, though, to pick out the colours for carpets, counter tops, walls and all those things. I had some extras installed, like a Jacuzzi and a double layer of carpet padding and things like that.

I wanted as much light in the place as I could muster. I don't like walls, so on one of our trips to the National Home Show, I met a guy who installed glass wall mirrors. Since there were several of these stalls, I tried out where I could get the best for the price I had to pay and decided on a nice and ambitious young guy who had just started his own business and was eager to have the business!

I arranged for him to see the condominium, and he arrived at the half of May. I decided which walls were to be mirrored, then I decided that since there were so many spaces that were left open for no reason and I could always do with more closet space, I would utilize his time and efforts and tell him I wanted to have an extra cupboard in the bedroom. Because of my empty space he made up a cupboard at my instructions for sweaters, blouses and such. Another open space in the bathroom was utilized, and he installed a linen cupboard there.

I had him install some shelves and cupboards up on the wall, and that included the top of my desk, which in the new condominium was in my way and blocked part of my beautiful view. I had him install it upside down on the wall in the computer room, thus creating an extra open cupboard.

He told me he had never met anybody that was as inventive as I was, because I even had him install a contraption under the bathroom sinks so that there were two shelves instead of just the bottom ones, and a drawer on the bottom to put small stuff! I changed the racks in the walk-in closet so that I have twice the space other people have in their units.

When I have people come to my place they ask whose ideas these were, because they don't have these things in their condominium!

Because the livingroom set I had did not fit in the new condominium, and since my son and his wife had just moved into a house rather than a dingy apartment and needed a new livingroom set, I made them happy and gave them mine. I bought a new set with slightly different colours and smaller, so everything would fit. Of course, at the same time I made Ash happy at Leon's with another sale!

Since I was there already, and I wanted another kitchen set, I picked one out that had the barstools with a high table. It looks quite nice in the kitchen. I gave the other set to Brenda, who was also quite happy with it!

On one of my trips to the mall I was fascinated by the blinds that one company was selling and displaying. They were all handpainted and made to suit each owner, and you could pick out your own style and the pictures you wanted. I had them over at my place, and Bernie happened to be visiting me at the time, so we picked out all the different scenes I wanted for each room.

The livingroom has a beautiful waterfall with a forest around it; the bedroom has an island style in all burgundy colours, with palms and little boats; the solarium, or cat room, has a jungle scene with two cats; the computer room, or second bedroom, has a Caribbean scene with lots of ocean and little islands and boats in the foreground; the kitchen has a Japanese scene with flowers and a bonsai tree. So you can see I put a lot of effort into this place!

# Chapter 8
# The Cruises

The first time I went on a cruise I was kind of scared. But Tom told me all would be well and that there was nothing to be afraid of, that nothing bad was going to happen. Of course not. The devil had me already in his back pocket, so what could go wrong?

Besides that, the infatuation that Tom had for me was probably all over by then, so all was well as far as he was concerned.

On the first of the cruises I went on we were all lying by the pool, and I wanted to take a dip to cool off. I was told, via thought control, that this was not a good idea and I should stay out of the water. I just dangled my feet over the side, and it was actually a good idea to stay out. The water came from the ocean and was ice cold! We were in the Atlantic Ocean, and it is a lot colder there than in the Pacific Ocean. Since we had started in Acapulco and were on our way to San Juan in Puerto Rico, there was a dramatic change in temperature because the Atlantic Ocean had just had a bad storm, so sweaters were needed after we got through the Panama Canal.

On one of the cruises we went to the Cayman Islands, and we were walking on the road to a place called, believe it or not, "Hell." It was not even a town, but two houses and a little store where you could buy things like "I have been to Hell and Back" souvenirs and things like that.

They also had a fun guillotine with a hole for your head and your arms to stick through. We all took each other's pictures from that and bought some stuff in the store. Like other times I was always the last one out!

But as we were walking outside a ramshackle house and heading toward the ship, a woman came out and looked at me, smiled, walked over and said, " I have waited for you. I heard you were coming." I thought nothing of it and told her I was glad to meet her finally and hoped she would have a good day. And don't ask me where these words came from either. I didn't know her from Adam and had no idea what I was talking about. She was very obviously a witch. She wore a long open skirt, and her garter belt was quite obviously in sight.

I think she made sure I saw it, and I had been looking at them in the store but did not buy them because we were with a bunch of people. I was afraid, that somebody would have seen it, but nobody had seen this exchange. I was held back at the store and was walking behind the rest, so nobody saw this exchange happening.

I realize now that my being held up in the store had a definite purpose, but I also think I was supposed to buy one of those garter belts there!

Another time I was walking back to the ship with our group and there was a woman standing there who just looked me over, smiled, nodded and turned back in the house.

At other times there were people who would just pass by me, brush my hand or something like that, and walk on as if they somehow knew me! Most of the time these were things that happened while I was on cruises. But there were plenty of those things happening in Toronto too.

We went on another trip to Cuba, and we were having a drink when this guy came up and told me he had something for me. Right away I started thinking of drugs, but he came up with this crazy shaped candle that I found out later was a sign for witches. He told me that it was for me and that he had held on to it to give to me. I am not the kind of person who collects these kind of things, but again I thought nothing of it and accepted it.

On another trip in Barbados we were walking around in the marketplace when, at one of the stalls, a woman looked at me and said she had something special for me. She came out with a beautiful muumuu that I just couldn't resist. The colours were so vibrant, and she practically gave it to me for free. I think I paid about five dollars U.S. for it!

Another time we were in Barbados and were walking along the street. There was a stall where they were selling opened coconuts that they filled with rum and coconut milk, and the guy said mine was for free but the others had to pay!

Since we had several cruises with the same people, they always asked me why I was always getting the good stuff. They would hang around me, but it didn't happen for them, but for me there was a special perk every time! And don't think that all these people were possessed by the devil, because he can use anybody he feels like using! It can be your best friend or your worst enemy!

*The devil will use anything or anybody. Don't ever forget that!*

I have seen so many beautiful islands and seen so many beautiful things, incredible sunrises and sunsets so indescribably beautiful, scene after scene after scene of incredible beauty, and flowers so gorgeous. We went on Isla de Margarita to an orchid garden; the scent and the beauty of the flowers was so fantastic that taking mere pictures didn't do it justice. But that is all one can do!

On one of my cruises we were in Isla de Marquarita again and visited a jewelry shop there that I had been to before. There was a beautiful black pearl ring, and I happened to look at the price and asked the girl if it was $8 U.S., and she said after she looked at the price tag that it was $8, so I of course put it on my finger, handed her $10, and she was just giving me the change when the manager rushed over and told her it was not $8, but rather $800! But I did get it for $8, got the change back from the ten, and I happily went on my way! If that would happen to me now I would realize that I have no business taking advantage of a situation like that and getting the other person into trouble. But at that time my thinking was, Too bad! Her loss, my gain!

I still always had this feeling of thanking God for nice and beautiful things like sunrises, sunsets and beautiful panoramas. That was never taken from me. I don't even know if that *could* have been taken away from me! I think I have such a beautiful guardian angel, who kept on reminding me that God was still there!

We also went to Stingray Island, where we went in shuttle boats and then got into the water. It was very shallow there, and we could actually pick up the stingrays and hold them and have pictures taken with them in our arms.

It was a very popular place, and we had a blind couple with us on board. This guy did everything we were doing, including dancing with his wife, who was pregnant. He told me that nothing was keeping them from having a good time, and he was living it up! I had several times taken pictures of them that he asked me to take, so we got to talking a bit. I handed him a stingray and then took pictures of him and his wife.

# Chapter 9
# The Devil at Work

Sometimes the feeling inside me was taken away to teach me a lesson, and I would feel so utterly unloved and alone that I would cry. I guess the purpose was so that I would miss it, and by wanting it back again I would be more than willing to behave the way I was supposed to! And I tell you, that worked like a charm!

But whenever I was on a cruise that feeling would always be there. During the nights I would be programmed that Tom was always with me wherever I went, and that this was his way of showing me he was always with me and loved me!

Twice I met a guy on one of the cruises, and both times he looked just like Tom. Of course, this was also a reminder to make sure I was in the right frame of mind and to not forget him! And these two guys were literally thrown at me for the purpose of a reminder! There would be no two ways about even trying to change my behaviour!

One time I had an apparition in the form of a young boy about twelve years old or so, who manifested himself in my window on the outside. He had a beautiful smile on his face, and I imagine his origin must have been from India or Pakistan.

He was hovering in the air in a frame, but I could see the lights from the mall through the picture, so I knew it was not a framed photograph. I was on the eighth floor at the time and there are no balconies where I live, so nobody could have dangled it over the balcony. The building is 34 stories high, so that wasn't very likely, but I didn't feel threatened. We sort of just stared at each other for about five minutes, but he did not move and neither did I. I suddenly thought, "This is ridiculous!" I walked away, but when I turned around he was still there, so I walked to the kitchen, which had an open concept. When I looked at the window again, he was gone.

What I didn't realize was that this was part and parcel of all the trouble I had gotten myself into, without even realizing, that I was already in deep trouble! It was meant, I guess, as a perk to show what I could look forward to! And you know, I really thought I was so privileged by all these kinds of things. The devil can really make you believe anything he wants to!

My thinking was so totally controlled and so programmed to believe anything that happened, that I just didn't think anything about it anymore and just took everything that was happening in and around me more and more for granted.

And the most frightening thing is that I was so much under Satan's control that I didn't know what to do when for one or other reason they took it away. They would do that every once in a while to show me the power he had over me. I would feel absolutely lost and would walk around in circles and would wring my hands and ask what should I do. I would beg them to please let me know if I had done something wrong so I could correct it.

I would cry and ask for them to please give me that feeling back, that I was lost without it and that I couldn't think straight anymore. It was absolutely true, you know, that the devil did control my mind to that extent. I didn't know even realize it and was totally at a loss of what to do at that point.

Then I was first made to totally surrender, and I would get another session, as it was called, to re-program me. This could also be in the middle of the day, when I would be marshaled back home and would go to bed. After that I would feel all right again!

But after each of these sessions I was made to feel more and more dependent on these feelings and would be made to feel totally dependent on them for my existence. After a while it became so automatic that I pretty well knew the drill by heart. But then something would be changed, and it was all different again!

At one of the sessions I was told to keep my right arm beside me with my palm down and my left arm upward besides me with the palm up. This I was told was so I could pick up any messages from outside with the fingers of my left hand, while the fingers of my right hand would retain the information inside of me. I had no idea that these were actually used to butt into people's lives.

I would also be made to hold my hand on top of my head and put the other one over it and keep them there till I was told to take them away. When I took them away there was also a special way to do this, and I had to sort of wipe them over my face going down to my shoulders and then keep them outstretched at my sides in supplication or surrender.

At other times I was made to put my index fingers over my eyes, than my nose, my mouth, my ears and my throat, than again in total surrender with my arms outstretched. Always after these things I had to surrender myself. At one time my hands with fingers bent apart were put on top of my head and then three times up and down on my head as if they were sort of imprinted on or in my head.

Sometimes my feet were separated and then my arms would be outstretched in surrender, and I would stay like that for a few minutes or longer, and then my feet would be pulled together so that my knees were totally apart and my feet bottoms together. I never found out what all this meant. It could very well be that these were only for show to make sure I knew who was in control. It went so automatically that I never thought anything of it, just took for granted that it was necessary and that was it! And all of this went under Tom's name!

But I got to look forward to these sessions and felt so good about them. I guess I was supposed to feel that way, so the change from freedom to total surrender to the devil was actually made pleasant and was so subtle that I was ensnared before I realized it!

At other times I was meant to feel bad with a headache, sore throat or something or other, and I was kept in bed the whole day or a whole weekend. These were the times I guess that Tom didn't want me around anywhere where he was.

The next morning I was taken to the mall again. This time it was early in the morning before banking hours, and I had coffee with Tom. By this time I was doing things automatically as was expected of me. I was an easy target, I can tell you!

The day after that I had to pick up something at the mall, so back I was again. Believe it or not I stayed there the whole day; it seemed I did not have any inclination to go anywhere else.

I had coffee and lunch with Tom again, and I more or less stayed around the mall and the bank. He was saying that divorces happened in their circles too, so I was quite happy!

Looking back on it now, of course, I realize that it was following the pattern that slowly but surely lets the devil cause you to lose all sense of proportion. You do automatically what is expected of you, and all you are is a zombie!

One day I was driving to the mall, and all of a sudden my car stopped functioning in the middle of the road for no reason. Since everything in a Cadillac is automatic, the steering stopped too and I could not move anything but was driving toward a hydropole. I screamed, and then the car stopped totally. I turned the ignition off and turned the key again, started the car, and there was nothing wrong.

When I told this story to Tom he said, "You must have done something wrong to deserve that reaction. Search your mind and find out where you went wrong." I had no idea what he was taking about and dismissed the whole episode from my mind.

During the night sessions I got to know that I had done something on my own, which was an absolute no-no. I was to do in future just what I was programmed for and not to try any stuff on my own, otherwise I would be very sorry!

After that there was more brainwashing, and I really did nothing on my own anymore! But that is all one can do! I was programmed to the extent that even the conversations were programmed in my mind that I was going to have the next day, what to say, what to do, how to react, where to go, what to wear. You name it, it was programmed. And you know what is so amazing? I absolutely thought nothing of it, and I thought that this was quite normal and there was nothing wrong with it!

Sometimes he would program me only partly. For instance, he would leave out what I was to wear and, believe it or not, I would be totally lost and couldn't find a thing to wear. I would be totally disoriented and would feel so lost that I would just ask Tom what I should do! Then, of course, the devil would show me what to wear and all was right with the world again as far as I was concerned!

And you know, the devil made me feel quite proud of the fact that I was being programmed. He made me feel that I was elevated in the world by these sessions of programming, and I thought it was the best thing that had ever happened to me!

All the girls in the bank always had smiles on their faces and were always so pleasant. There was never a bad word or a long face; they were all influenced by the same thing, and I think that was done before the bank opened and Tom was in. He would have a meeting to boost their morale, as he called it, all for the glory of Tom. And I must admit, he was a good manager. The bank was doing extremely well, but everything was manipulated in cahoots with the devil!

Believe me, it can be done. You would have nothing to say about it. It was the same thing with the car. It was driving me wherever they wanted me to go, and there was nothing I could do about it. I also did not want to do anything about it; the car was driving me rather than me driving it.

Sometimes I was taken to spots where he had other women waiting for him, and I guess I was sent there to check whether they were actually there and waiting for him. I know that is what happened, because he has done the same to me at times.

Once he had me waiting for two and half hours somewhere only to come rushing by in somebody else's car. What I didn't know was they were coming from Peterborough on a Sunday afternoon, and I was left standing there just because he wanted to show me off to his friends!

In the summertime I was driven most of the time on the weekends to the Peterborough area, where Tom had a trailer. I would be driving around there for a couple of hours and then would be driven home again. After a while I expected it and just fell into the trap, because as Tom pointed out, wasn't it nice and easy that I didn't have to worry about anything and everything got done.

All my weekends were arranged. Either that or I would spent them in bed "not feeling well." I never had to worry about things, and if sometimes nothing was arranged I would yell and holler and then I would be driven to a park or somewhere else where I could sit in the sun.

I was taught while driving to use my "powers," which were slowly given to me in small doses to keep me happy. I could ask people on the road to politely and safely get out of my way so I could have the road clear before me. This worked like a charm most of the time.

Sometimes I got a car in front of me that couldn't care less who was driving behind them, but most of the time they moved to the other lane!

When I think back on things, I think the people that did not get out of my way where probably religious. The devil could not get through to them!

I was also introduced to some of Tom's friends, and I was so proud of that!

I always found that I was made to buy stuff before I needed it, and would find out a little later that it was a good thing I had bought it, because it was exactly what I needed!

# Chapter 9
# The Wedding

One night there was a session in which I was made Tom's wife. This was after hearing that divorces also happened in their circles, and that made me so happy!

That was the day after one of the sessions where I had to blank my mind. When they changed my mind even more to their way of thinking, I again was marshaled to the mall where Tom was sitting with another witch. He stood up and looked in the direction from where I was coming. He said, "My wife is coming to join me." Oh, I felt in seventh heaven hearing that from his lips!

When we left he first ticked the other witch on the shoulder and then did the same to me. I felt so proud because he changed the relationship from her to me, and I could feel her resentment. But I just thought, Her loss, my gain! Can you believe that?

The night sessions were going pretty well each and every night. They were mostly to change my thinking and also to inform me when things around me were changing or to make changes in my body without my knowledge. It was also to indoctrinate me in various things they wanted to use me for.

If I wouldn't get a night session I would ask what the matter was, because it became so much of a ritual that I needed it to feel secure again!

These were things I noticed after they had been done and I became aware of these changes. They were not always to my advantage, of course, but I didn't know this until it was too late. I couldn't do anything about it anyway!

Everything was regimented, even including when to get up in the morning, what time to go to bed, when I was to do the laundry, when to shop, when to clean, what to buy, the food I ate, and the clothes I wore. I never had to think where I was going, because I would just be taken there.

Sometimes I would meet Tom on these shopping sessions, and we would shop together, which was a bonus for me. It didn't happen all the time, and we would spend some time together. Most of the time it was, I think, when the devil thought I needed a good dose of Tom again to keep me in line. Sometimes it was because Tom had a message for me, or the devil thought I was ready for an advancement in the program. There was always a reason! And of course I loved these meetings, because it was Tom showing his "love" for me, right? How dumb can you get?

# Chapter 10
# About Spaceships and Devils

I have also visited a spaceship, and that image is still very vivid in my imagination. I was thoroughly examined by a bunch of what I believe were doctors, because they were all dressed in white coats with stethoscopes and the whole bit.

This was done around midnight, and I was told to take all my clothes off and lie perfectly still and not move on my bed, except for breathing. By that time all I did was do as I was told.

I remember I was placed on a stretcher. We went through a long tunnel with lots of lights, and I ended up in a sort of operating room with a bunch of people around me. I was told to close my eyes. Somehow I still have this sensation that they were poking around in and around my body, and believe you me, I was checked out thoroughly, including my eyes, mouth, nose and ears. It was quite literally everything, but what they did I have no idea. Inside my body I could feel they were poking around, but then the devil can make you believe anything!

I have no idea what transpired, because the next thing I knew a couple of hours later I found myself in bed under the covers, but still naked. If this was a figment of my imagination then it was a good one, because I can still picture the whole scene in front of my eyes and can still feel them working on my body!

It is in a way as if I am reliving the whole scene!

There is a story of a fifteen-year-old boy who strangled his classmate. In the newspaper it states, and I quote, "It was also revealed that he had been reading *Mein Kampf*, had 'expressed racist views' and talked about 'astral traveling' and 'out-of-body experiences.'"

It sounds like this poor teenager is going through what I went through, except for the reading of *Mein Kampf*, which, having gone through the second World War, I would never ever have been able to read a book like that. Several times it was shoved under my nose, but I told them what to do with that book in a hurry! So even the devil knew his limits, apparently! I was never exposed to racism after that.

Since I had gotten to know the way Tom could change his features and manipulate things and people, I thought maybe he was an alien and was put here to impregnate the earth!

Never at any time did the thought come into my mind that it really was the devil that was at the bottom of the whole charade. They made sure that my thinking did not go in the direction of the devil, so I pictured all sort of things.

Of course, it was the devil that made me think things like that. Since I didn't know any better, all sorts of things were being put in my head except the truth!

There once was a robbery in the bank, and he "caught" the robber in the washroom. He said he recognized him by his runners. Likely story, isn't it? He caught him, but he probably told the devil, "Hey, you overdid your boundaries!" Or it was done to make him look good!

# Chapter 11
# Devil's Messenger

After a couple of years things started to change, and that is when I noticed this low, heavy voice started to come through during the night. I was told that this was a big advancement for me and that I should be very proud of it. I started talking in tongues and reverted Latin and all sorts of goodies!

Eventually after a while it was just part of the whole thing, and I didn't think twice about these nightly conversations anymore.

I have had all sorts of conversations between what I now know was Satan and what I always thought was Tom. Now I think it could have been anybody, and I had no idea who he was talking to. I was never told it was Satan when he was talking through me. I was also told that I really didn't have to know who it was and that I should just accept it as one of the things that had to be done.

He had this low, low voice that came out of the depths, and he mostly spoke in tongues at those times to use me to get through to others. I was told I was the best medium he had found in a long time, and I picked up people's minds faster than they had been able to before.

Sometimes I would talk or sing in reverted Latin during the night sessions, or I would hear a conversation between Satan and somebody else with a high voice, which I now believe was St. Michael. I could hear they were yelling at each other, but I have no idea who they were, come to think of it. Maybe they were fighting over my soul, I have no idea. I could never interrupt these arguments, because I was told in no uncertain terms by the devil to stay out of it, that it had nothing to do with me and to stay quiet, which I did!

Poor St. Michael! I must have given him a hard time through my ignorance!

But I was made to feel so very proud of the fact that I could be used for these things, so I never questioned these sessions anymore!

Besides that, Satan made sure I was in the right frame of mind for these sessions and had me surrender before and after each and every one of them! It was just another way to make sure I would stay under his thumb and cooperate!

I would get these images of murders, and sometimes he would use my body to show how someone was murdered and how they were mutilated. I could actually feel it and cry out in pain!

These were the bad sessions. After those I used to cry for that person, but would never know who it was, except once, where there was a girl missing. She was found in the pit of a quarry, and the night before that story was in the newspaper, Satan had shown me where she was thrown and how she had died. He even took me on the road that the guy had taken to drive her there and how she was thrown in the gravel pit like a bag of sand!

Another time there was this girl who was strangled, and I felt I was literally being strangled. I even made the gurgling noises and felt myself slipping away. Then I was taken out of it. It was used to show how much power he had over me and to keep me in line!

Another time were there were a couple of girls picked up off the road, but I don't know where that was, and I was shown how they were used by a couple of guys and then were killed! No, not everything was fun, but was done for intimidation. I tell you, it worked like a charm!

Sometimes I saw images of children, beautiful little girls, anywhere from five or six years old to about ten or eleven. They would just look at me as from a photograph or in a frame, and after a while they would just fade away. I have never been able to find out what this meant. The only thing I can think of in hindsight is that these poor children were used as sacrifices.

I have never recognized any of these children, so they were not from around here. Otherwise I would have seen pictures about them in the papers. After these nightly sessions I always checked the newspapers the next day, but nothing was ever mentioned.

What has always bothered me was the fact that there was a girl in my area that disappeared in June 1995 who was never heard of again. I think she was seventeen when she disappeared. Since it was around the time that I started to get involved with this terrible thing I have often wondered if it had anything to do with me. Not that I was part of the act, but maybe she was used as a sacrifice to get me to submit to Tom or actually Satan.

To do this kind of a powerful spell there had to be a sacrifice of some sort, and this has always bothered me deeply. It is a terrible thing to think of, but is the only thing I can come up with. After sessions like that I would scan the papers to see if there were any reference in it in the newspapers.

I realize now why these sessions that happened during the night never came up in conversations during the day with Tom. Tom probably didn't know anything about these sessions, because it had nothing to do with him. Unless the devil would tell him and then use him to make me believe the things that were happening within me. He probably only told him what had to be done, and that is why Tom sometimes reacted as a robot. He was just as much used by the devil as I was, except he was really changed into a devil and did it in full knowledge of what he was doing!

If you think of the things the devil can do to you and to your body, it is so scary that it would keep you running to God for everything under the sun. That is as it should be!

One day we were walking outside, and Tom told me there was a reason for this exercise. We went to the back of the mall and there were a bunch of kids around ten or eleven years old fooling around. Tom said, "Oh, look! Those we call ankle biters." The kids were too far away from us to hear us, but some went down on the ground and started biting the other girls' ankles! And this was done with just a twist of his wrist! Talk about power…when you can get a bunch of kids to do something like that!

Another time I was at his house, just talking on the driveway with him. He had retired by this time, and I was driven to his place. His wife still worked, so it was all right, and he told me he would be right back. When he was walking back to me I had my back to him, and I felt this jolt in my back. I turned around, and he just shrugged his shoulders and told me he was going inside, so I left.

After that I got the worst backache I have had in a long time! I guess he didn't really want me around and gave me the pain as a revenge for showing up at his place. That is when I told him to stop getting me to be driven around his place, because I didn't like that either! But it kept on being a part of the procedures!

# Chapter 12
# The Branding

There was one time when I was having a birthday party for my son, and I was cooking the noodles. Bernie was standing next to me when all of a sudden a splash of the boiling water just kind of jumped out of the pan and burned my hand. I think it freaked Bernie out, because he was helping me and it was such a weird thing the way it happened. The children got all upset, and we had no idea where the water came from because, as we said, it literally came out of the blue! The funniest part of it was that while it looked bad, I hadn't felt a thing when it happened and never felt anything after that either! But we bandaged it, and I kept happily going on.

The next day I was, of course, with Tom in his office, and I mentioned it to him.

He said, "Oh, so you have finally been branded by the looks of it. I hope it was done right!"

I said something like, "Oh, is that what it was? I never felt anything."

He said, "Let me have a look at it," so I took the bandage off. He then said, "Oh, this was not done right, this one won't even leave a

scar. It will have to be done again. You have to be properly branded."
I asked him when that would be, but he said I wouldn't have to know,
so I wouldn't be upset when it happened again.

He also didn't like where it was done. He said it had to be another
spot where it would be more noticeable! And I was so proud of the
fact that I was branded. I wanted that scar so badly! I can't believe
that I ever would have that kind of reaction!

I had a small electronic game that I played off and on. One time I
had the cleaning lady in, and she called me to the bathroom and said,
"Look at your game!" And that thing was just going a mile a minute
and could not be stopped. It was being programmed, believe it or not!
The next day when I played that game I won and had the highest score
of four thousand points. Every time I played it after that I would get
high numbers and things would always turn out in my favour!

But if I did something wrong that would be taken away from me,
and I was let known that I had done something wrong. Believe it or
not I would actually apologize! The hold the devil had over me was
just unbelievable, and it took a long time to come to the surface that
it was Satan and nothing else.

One time I was taken to my computer and started typing a letter to
Tom. It was just a nonsense thing, and I had a lot of fun just typing
away. I was just making joking remarks, and after a while I stopped
writing and my fingers started typing like crazy. Out came the reply
to my letter to Tom! I had been typing away, and it was actually his
reply to my letter! That was so much fun, because it seemed like I was
getting replies and we were just joking back and forth!

I thought this was great, and it went on for a long time. I had a ball
with it, and it all seemed so real. I was in seventh heaven, I tell you!
But I was also told never to make copies of them and to delete
everything at the end of the day. But sometimes I did not do that, and
I copied them anyway. Now I have thrown them all out, though.

When Tom didn't want to talk to someone or let them come close
to him, he had a particular way of standing with one knee bent and the
other sort of backwards, and the person would actually turn around
and walk away.

I have done it on occasions too when I saw him and he was talking to someone and didn't want to be interrupted! It was as if he barricaded himself against any other person than the one he was talking to, and I was just marshaled away and had no say in the matter. At first I didn't know what was going on, but then I thought, Let me see what happens if I do go over. Well, I did that once, but never again; the fury was so potent that I never wanted to do that again!

And it was not that it was a setup. In reality he wanted to let me know how much power he had so I would be thoroughly impregnated with the idea that he could do anything, to scare me into staying with the program. It also let me know that if I would not do what he wanted me to do that he had ways to make it happen!

But these powers could eventually become my powers too! I met a queen witch, and she had power! Oh, yes, they know how to get you!

# Chapter 13
# The Devil's Protection Against Intruders

I once, through a friend, met a guy who wanted a date with me. I thought, Why not? It's free dinner! So I went, but I didn't know that this was also a guy into Satanism. I had a nice extended lunch with him and went home via the mall, of course, and we tentatively set up a date for the next day.

Tom was waiting for me and was talking to what I know now to have been Satan, and he made me listen to the conversation. Satan was told in this case to do something about one situation, that it was not to be tolerated, and that it had to be acted upon right away! The next day the guy I had had lunch with before told me he couldn't see me any more and cancelled the date we had for lunch. He said his brand-new car was totaled the night before! And I was actually proud of the fact that I thought Tom loved me so much that he had this done for me, or so I was believed to think!

For that I was punished too. I got a fungus infection in my nails that just about destroyed them. They have never been the same since, although now they are starting to look natural again under God's careful and tender loving care!

I also met one of his other friends, who banked at the same place and who wanted to take me out for coffee. I have never seen him since then! I guess he was told to stay away too. I was already in the bag!

Sometimes I was taken to where there was a bad accident. I never knew what it had to do with me, unless it was to show me what could happen to me if I didn't do as I was told or programmed for.

The night sessions became very frequent, and each time I changed yet a little bit more without realizing it. I think sometimes I was marshaled home and felt so tired during the day that I went to bed and fell asleep, only to wake up a couple of hours later. I think these were times that Tom did not want me in the mall or around him, and I was just taken away from the area!

# Chapter 14
# The Acquisition of My "Familiar"

One time the idea was planted in my head that I had to have two cats, one black, to be my familiar, and the other should be white.

I went to a pet shop and saw this cute, tiny little black fur ball, and I instantly fell in love with that tiny little thing. When the girl came over I told her that I wanted a white one as well. They had only one little white fluffy fur ball with a raccoon tail, and I thought it was the cutest little thing I had ever seen. I said, "Let's see if they like each other." We put them together in the room we were in and right away the black one, Donner, started licking the white one, Blitzen. I told her not to separate them any more, and they were okayed by the veterinarian. The next day I picked them up.

They are very cute and nice cats and very healthy, but I think I have to pass them on.

Donner, which was the black one, was possessed. He really *was* my familiar and was always around me when I was home. He jumped on my shoulder when I was in bed, or he would be at my feet, curled up against me.

When I went out, and that was quite frequent, he would be sitting at the door when I came home and would follow me everywhere. He can play like a dog, he will retrieve, he even kicks the ball and brings it to me. He used to curl up against me like a man would do and be so loving; it was incredible!

While I am writing away here, Donner is constantly hanging around me and is bothering me. You see, that is the devil at work, because Donner would normally be asleep on my bed by now. The poor cat was sent to distract me! So you can see how writing this book is not easy for me and that it can cause problems. I have such a battle of soldiers rooting for me that I am not really afraid; I just have to be careful. I think I frightened the devil away!

The two of them are still very close, but Donner would let me know if someone was at the door or the phone was ringing and I didn't hear it. He would have a way to remind me of things that had to be done, and I got so used to it that now I sometimes think, Gee, he doesn't do this or that anymore!

But now I think he is still being used by the devil as a channel to me, and so I have to get rid of them to keep my sanity! This morning I was talking to someone on the phone and mentioned that I thought Donner was still being used as a channel by the devil, and I thought I had better find a good home for them. He came literally begging on his knees and came crawling to me! When I asked him what he was doing, he quit doing it and acted normal again! I am not meant to have them anymore, and I don't need them anymore. Besides that, I have so many things to do now that I really don't have enough time for them. That is not fair to the cats either.

# Chapter 15
# More Devilry

I have, of course, a scapular. The first one I had I forgot to put it on one morning before going to Mass, and when I came home Donner was hiding from me and acting funny. I took off my coat and went to the bedroom and just about had a fit!

I have a very special statue of Mama Maria that was blessed by the Pope in the seventies when my father had an audience with the Pope and had this statue especially blessed for my mother. After she passed away, I got it! Well, I had hung the scapular over the statue of Mama Maria. The statue was knocked over, everything in sight was knocked over, and the *leather* scapular lay in two pieces on my dresser! I ran over, but the statue was not broken, Thank God!

So I put everything together again and got myself a new scapular and had it blessed for sure. The first one was also blessed in Nebraska on a pilgrimage.

I have a small statue of St. Michael and one of Mama Maria standing on my television. When I came home from church one afternoon after I had been selling raffle tickets for the Easter draw, I looked at the television and couldn't find the St. Michael statue. The holy Mary statue had fallen over.

The St. Michael statue had fallen, and I have no idea how it ended up there on the bottom shelf inside a cabinet where the television is standing! That is an acrobatic feat, I can tell you! The arm was broken, so I got my crazy glue out and fixed it right away. I have sprinkled both statues with holy water.

I have no idea when this happened. It could have happened the day before, but it should not have happened at all. It could not have happened the way it did unless somebody threw it underneath in the shelf. Believe you me, I did not do that! I have got an idea that either Donner was thrown against it when I wasn't home, or it was thrown by the devil because he doesn't like at all what I am doing right now. He lets it be known!

So even now that everything is blessed and sprinkled with holy water, things can still happen. That is how dangerous the devil is!

So stay clear of him at all times. Whenever you get anything that comes to you during the night, make the sign of the cross right away and be very aware that you absolutely do not ask what is happening. Reject it right away without questions asked, because one question asked is one too many. By that time you are already in the devil's hands, so no questions, no conversation at all, because you don't want to go there! Just ask God for protection against the evil spirit that is around you, and ask St. Michael to protect you. Start praying right away and don't forget to make the sign of the cross and take a rosary or a cross in your hands for protection, because it is a certainty that this spirit is Satan. It does not come from God, who is light, but comes from the devil, because he does everything under the cover of darkness. He shuns the daylight as much as possible.

I will write the Prayer of St. Michael here below for the people who do not know it:

> St, Michael, the archangel, defend me in battle; be my defense against the wickedness and the snares of the devil. May God rebuke him, we humbly pray, and do thou, oh prince of the heavenly host, by the power of God, thrust into hell Satan and all the evil spirits who prowl about the world, seeking the ruin of souls.

There are also people that do not like the daylight, and they generally work during the night and sleep through the day. If they tell you they can't stand the sunlight or are too sensitive to the sunlight, be very aware of them, because they could be vampires. I have met a couple of those too, so don't let anybody tell you that they don't exist!

There are a lot of things we do ourselves that make the work of the devil very easy, you know! I am talking about the ones that they call schizophrenic. Most of the time the devil can be exorcized if somebody would just get the right idea!

It is so dreadful to see people who could be totally normal being possessed by the devil when they could be exorcized and lead a normal and full life instead being on drugs. Drugs only numb the brain and makes zombies out of them! It kills their creativity, and they can't function the way they're used to.

# Chapter 16
# The Necessity

After reading this book I think you will have gotten the picture why this book is so necessary in this age and why people have to be educated on this subject. There is so much of it going on, and it is quite rampant in every part of the globe, no matter where you live.

Since I trusted Tom completely (and as far as banking was concerned, he was to be trusted), I let all these other things happen to me and let them do as they wanted with me, all in the name of Tom. Of course, it was since he was the love angle for me in this case.

I would hear from others during the next day as confirmation of what had happened. For instance, when they made me a witch I heard it from a friend the next day that I had been initiated during the night by the devil, which of course I thought of as being Tom!

And you know what the most unbelievable thing is? I was quite proud of the fact that I was now a witch. I saw myself as a good witch that still believed in God as well! I think sometimes he made me go to church just to show God how far I was under his control! Show-off time! How that must have hurt God!

Slowly but surely, Tom showed me what he was capable of. I tell you, there was not much he could not do. At that time I didn't know as yet, but he was known in their circles as the wizard, which is the highest rank you can achieve. He was constantly talking to the devil.

Sometimes he made me walk beside him just so it wouldn't be too obvious he was talking to Satan. To other people in the mall it would look like he was talking to himself, and so he wouldn't look like a lunatic he often used me as a decoy. And I was so proud of that! I thought, Wow, he is talking to other people (at that time I still had no idea it was the devil he was talking to), and he doesn't mind that I listen in.

After a couple of months of this stuff and being so thoroughly initiated into the whole program, I was elevated to queen witch one night. This was also an incredible night. I automatically took out my new white robe set (for whatever reason I didn't know), but that is what I did. I was made to buy this set previously on one of my many shopping expeditions.

Since it was a full moon I opened the blinds. It was the end of October, which is the harvest moon, and the most powerful one, especially if it falls on Halloween. I got the feeling and the thought to go with it that I needed the full moon shining on me, so I was made to stay perfectly still on my bed and let the moon shine into my wide, open eyes. I was kept there with my eyes focused on the moon and told not to say a word. You know, I even felt and saw the moon rays coming toward me, and I could feel them washing over my body!

After a while I was made to get up and undress and stand close to the window. Since there were no lights on in my place I didn't have to be afraid of anybody looking in from the street below. I doubt if I would have been allowed to think that. I let the moon shine on me. I had to have my hands in the air so the moon rays would penetrate my whole being, and I would become inundated with the moon and would feel part of it so that it would stay with me. Then I was made to bow before the moon, and I was literally made to ask for power from the moon goddess. After that I was always looking forward for the moon. It is incredible how vulnerable you can become and how easily obsessed the devil can make you for certain things.

Then I was made to lie down on my bed again. My feet were pulled apart so the moon could penetrate my inner being, and I was kept in this position for a long time. Then there was this conversation between a bunch of guys. Someone with a very low voice, which I thought was Tom, and someone else were yelling really loud and hard. That could have been St. Michael fighting for me to get me back. When I think back on it, it makes sense, but at the time I had no idea this would even be a possibility.

That yelling went on for quite a while at a conference, and someone was asking questions to which they had to answer. They were discussing me, and I heard what I believed was Tom talking on my behalf. I was told just to keep quiet and not to say a word. After half an hour or so I was told to surrender, and with that gesture I sealed my fate. Because of the feeling that was stirred inside of me I couldn't do anything else but give the answers Satan was looking for and wanted so badly!

I was asked if becoming a queen witch was what I wanted, and I had to answer, "Yes, I do." Then I was told that I had to be programmed differently for this, and I was asked if hat was what I wanted. I said yes again, so they programmed me again. Then we had another session, but I can't remember all the questions that were asked.

I know one of the questions was about whether I would let them do whatever was necessary to make things work for me. Once I had agreed to those conditions, and after I had given all my answers, I was told that now I was installed as a queen witch. Everyone congratulated me, so I was what they called re-programmed. There was another love session as celebration; I felt so honoured.

I felt part of the whole operation even though I never went to these night sessions. I was driven to the general areas where they were held, but never was actually on the premises.

Although I think I was meant to be at some of them, I was always driven away from them again for some reason. I think now that that was probably a good thing!

# Chapter 17
## The Queen Witch

The next day one of my friends said, "There is the queen!" Was I ever proud of that! Several people that day said the same thing. One guy in a bookstore I went to with a friend of mine came over to where we were and took my arm and said, "If the queen is ready, we can proceed."

He took us to the cashier, and my girlfriend, who was the witch I talked about earlier, held up the cape from the outfit I was wearing and said she was my lady-in-waiting! She confirmed once again what had transpired the night before.

I knew this girl, Gitta, in 1995. She was a manicurist, and she always did my nails. She started working somewhere else, and I followed her because she was good at her job. We got along together pretty good. Well, believe it or not, after two manicures I noticed she did not look so good and was not as groomed as she used to be. I asked Gitta what was wrong with her, and she said nothing, that everything was all right. I could see there was something wrong, but let it pass. There was not much I could do about it if she didn't want to talk.

When I think back on it now, I think that Irma told her she was a witch and spooked poor Gitta!

The next week when I went back her boss told me that Gitta all of a sudden didn't show up for work anymore and that was that. Irma was helping me that day, and when she started working on my feet she said out of the blue, "I am a witch, you know."

I thought she was joking and answered, "Well, I call myself a bitch sometimes."

But she kept on insisting she was a real witch. All of a sudden I was prompted to say, "You know, Tom is my bank manager."

She looked at me, walked away from me, and then I heard her saying with a laugh in her voice, "Oh Tom, you got there first!"

What I didn't realize at the time was that they knew each other. I, of course, was quite proud of the fact, but it also confirmed the story I was meant to believe that it was indeed Tom and not Satan that was in control of me.

She was in a coven, and they always get together either in Florida or Arizona, where they would assemble. She told me all about it, but although I was meant to join a coven, I was never installed anywhere. Tom, or Satan, did not seem to want me in one. Arizona is a very bad spot for Satanism. I know of several families who are into this thing in that area.

I have met other witches, but one was a queen witch who invited me to a family affair. I don't think I was supposed to go there at that time, because I passed her place without going in. They also had a lot of money. It looks good, but it is better to be poor than in the hands of Satan!

After I was installed as queen witch I noticed that I wasn't programmed anymore, so I was told that things had changed and that I was now on a different and higher level. Programming was not necessary anymore; it was done on a different scale.

I was told to breathe deeply, to imagine myself standing on the top of a spiral staircase and going down the staircase. I was to go down the steps while counting to five and saying, "Deeper psychic level" with each step. That way I would go to a lower subconscious level so that my body would be more relaxed.

As time went on I had to count to six, seven, eight, even nine, ten and eleven. What I didn't know was that also lowers your whole system to the extent that sometimes I got quite dizzy. Since I was in bed I really didn't notice it that much.

What I didn't realize was that this was a far more dangerous level, because now the devil was even more potent than before. I was totally disarmed in such a way that my mind was totally taken over. My whole personality was changing because he was working on my subconscious level and just changed whatever he felt like changing!

I noticed one time that my mouth would change as if something was making me blow up my mouth, but from the inside. I could not open my mouth! That happened maybe four or five times in a row before I could open my mouth again. After that I noticed the next day that I started to swear and curse. I got to be more vocal and bad tempered. I started to say nasty things to people, which is not my nature at all, and I started to be very intolerable.

I hated when these things happened, but there was nothing I could do about it. After these things I also noticed that I could do things that I couldn't do before.

Then to make up for the fact that he had more power over me than before, and I let this happen, I was kind of compensated. I would be taken to a store and to find something special, or I would get an invitation for lunch or dinner, or all of the sudden I would notice that I got compliments from everyone I met. People would actually go out of their way to let me have my way.

I always would be driven to an empty parking spot when I needed one. I never had to look for a parking spot; there would always be a spot for me! When I wanted or needed something, I got the best there was and was driven to it, or it would come my way somehow! That is the way the devil works! It keeps you in check and happy.

Now I remember that Tom had a sign on his car, and I asked him what it was. He said that it was a sign that implied you worked things from your instinct. But it was not his instinct but the devil that made him do all the things he was doing. Since that time he has bought a new car, and now that sign is hidden under the hood of the car so no one can see it anymore!

At different times they let me listen in on people's conversations while I was in my own place and they were in theirs. Mostly I heard these conversations during the nightly sessions. I have heard conversations between my sisters and brothers and their spouses in Holland while I was in Canada.

I have listened to conversations between husband and wife, I have seen things that happen in households between husband and wife without knowing who they were or where they were.

I have heard conversations between families, arguments, fights and lovemaking. I have seen people walking in a mall without knowing who they were, but they were shopping, and I saw which store they went to. Then I would see another picture from the mall, mostly taken from above. It seemed to me as if I was hovering over the mall and was just watching the whole scene. You name it, it was done! All to impress on me how much I had to look forward to!

Or it could be that I was being trained to think these things were quite normal and to expect them from then on so I could butt in on people's conversations and actions without blinking an eye and think nothing of taking people's privacy away from them!

In the beginning I used to say that I didn't like to do these things, but always the next night I would be told to surrender, to go to a deep psychic level, and when I got out of these sessions I would think that the things I was doing were actually quite normal and a lot of fun. I would rationalize that no one was injured, so who cared? I would think that I was only expanding my horizons and using my instincts so that my brain capacity was only getting better.

I would actually just take it for granted after these sessions, because I would not even think about it anymore and it was just a part of my life. After awhile, and enough change in my personality, of course, I got used to that and even started to ask for them when they didn't happen. Now when I think I actually did these things I can't believe myself, and now I can't do them anymore. Thank You, God!

# Chapter 18
# Out-of-Body Experiences

There was one night that I was told to close my eyes and picture removing myself from my body and have a look at myself lying in bed. It worked like a charm. I looked at myself from the ceiling of my bedroom and saw myself lying in bed with my eyes closed!

Once when I thought I was talking to "Tom" during the night, he told me he was coming to pick me up because we were going on a tour around Ontario. I felt so happy and honoured by this. It was to be a night session, and he would keep me warm under his cape. He had the powers and I didn't, so I would come under his protection.

I was taken in the middle of the night, and it really looked like Tom who came to pick me up. I think it all happened without leaving my bed, but it seemed to me as if we were really flying all over not only Lake Ontario, where I would see the ships coming and going, but over Peterborough and over Toronto. I could see the traffic on the highways moving. I was shown places as seen from the air.

We were drifting over beautiful landscapes, and I would see them again when I closed my eyes. And I remember he actually came for me outside my window, and I went with him! I think that is where the witches' hour of flying to the moon came from, because it really feels and looks as if you are flying around outside!

Of course, the biggest changes were made on the full moon cycle. That is where I was really made to feel like a queen. All sorts of good things were happening then. Thinking back on these special sessions, they were the worst ones for me spiritually, because that is when the moon is at its fullest and the impact is far more pronounced. I could feel it too, because those were the times that I felt myself having the most power. It was a temporary thing, but it gave me the feeling that the time of the full moon was the most important part of the month. As long as I looked forward to the full moon, it would benefit me.

So every month I would look forward to the moon coming out. When it wasn't there, because of bad weather, I would feel kind of lost. How could I survive without the moon hovering over me? As soon as the moon would come back I was almost jubilant, and I would feel so utterly privileged that I wanted more and more of it! And that is exactly what the devil wants you to feel. I really did these things and thought that way!

# Chapter 19
# Time Out

Sometimes I got so tired, that I had to beg for time out to get some sleep. The nights were as busy as the day, and then I was bushed. But there were days that I was kept in bed to sleep and take things easy! I think they picked their times to have me around and then disbursed me when this was necessary. Most of the time I was around Tom's workplace, so I was in the mall.

One day I was also taken on a ride in my car. This is a reality, and it started in the morning around eleven. I began driving around, finally ending up in Ottawa, with the most incredible sunset I have ever seen. It lasted until close to 11 p.m., but before it started to disappear, it was so beautiful.

I was driven around and around in the same area all that evening, not knowing I was close to where Tom had his trailer. I needed gas and ended up in Ottawa after totally running out of gas. I could see the gas station across the river, but couldn't get to it. By this time it was close to 12 o'clock, and I was scared being alone at that time in a city I didn't know.

So I started yelling, at which I was getting very good and

increasingly better at. I was told to phone 911, but since the battery was on empty because I had not anticipated to be away so long, I didn't think I had a ghost of a chance. All of a sudden there was enough power to dial 911, so I got through. The girl that answered stayed with me until a cop came, who got enough gas for me to get me to the gas station.

He took me to the gas station and waited there till I was ready to go. He took me to the highway, and so I was finally on my way home. I was driven with a steady 160 k.m. home, and finally was home at 5:15 a.m.!

It was a beautiful trip, and I don't regret it at all! Since then I was taken on several trips, whenever and wherever Tom went out of Toronto for the weekend, I apparently had to go there too!

# Chapter 20
# The Trip to Holland

I forgot to mention that in July 1995 I had a trip planned to Holland, but Tom didn't really want me to go. I arrived at the airport and checked in, went aboard, and then the plane was delayed. There was some mechanical problem.

When we finally took off and were in the air, I was looking out of the window and said to the guy sitting next to me, "We are flying over Hamilton. I think we are going back to Toronto."

Then the captain came on the air and said, "Ladies and gentlemen, we are currently flying over Lake Ontario to lose gas. We will be flying back to Toronto because we have mechanical difficulties. Dinner will be served shortly, please do not take too long over it. We might not have enough time to serve dessert."

When we got close to Toronto I was happily playing with my electronic game. The captain came by and asked how I was doing. I told him I was fine, but then when we were close to Toronto, I said, "Wow, look at all these emergency vehicles!" We had ambulances, fire engines and cruisers all escorting our plane to its berth!

Of course, the first-class people disembarked first, and I was one of the first people out. I saw the Channel Nine people standing there, and I thought, Boy, this must really be something!

But we were safe and sound, so it was okay with me! I decided to go home, and when I got to my condominium I said to the people in the elevator jokingly, "Boy, that was a short holiday!"

They asked if I was on flight so and so, where the engine caught fire!

I could not believe it! On the upper deck where we were sitting you could not see it, but the people in economy class could. One of the people on the plane saw what was happening and had made a video of the whole affair and had sold the rights to Channel Nine before we disembarked.

I don't know how he got in touch with the Channel Nine people, but they were waiting at the entrance to the plane to receive the video when we landed, so it was already on the air by the time I was in my building.

Needless to say, my kids phoned me and left messages to get in touch with them right away and never mind the time of night! I phoned them all and reassured them that all was well and there was nothing to worry about!

The next day, after all the arrangements were made for the new flight, I got to the airport again only to find out that they had double-booked me on another flight that had left one hour earlier.

I showed them the one where they had booked me for, and they apologized all over the place and got me on another flight, which had a bunch of people from Ottawa on it also from the day before. They were all quite livid at having their vacation shortened by two days, because they had been on another flight that had been canceled due to mechanical problems. However, after one hour we had all safely boarded the plane. There seemed to be a bit of a problem with the captain's cabin.

Being in first class you get a glass of wine right away, and I was happily sipping away when we were going toward the runway. We are standing at the runway and the captain came on the intercom.

"Ladies and gentlemen, I am afraid I have to go back to our berth.

We have to get something checked out. Please remain in your seats, and the flight attendants will serve you a drink shortly."

I started to panic right away and said to the flight attendant, "I am getting off this plane. I probably was not meant to go to Holland. I am getting off here and now."

Well, she was a very good flight attendant. She sat down beside me, gave me a glass of wine and soothed me to the extent that I stayed on the flight to enjoy a good time in Holland.

When I was visiting my eldest sister for a couple of days, we were all sitting in the backyard when one of her daughters said to me, "You are a witch, aren't you?"

I just acknowledged it. I never got the chance to deny it, the words were already said before I even had a chance to think about the answer.

After I came back from Holland I told Tom what had happened with the plane I was on. He looked kind of funny at me and said, "I told you I didn't want you to go there!"

Every time I go over this book I come up with more stories, but then it can be too monotonous and too repetitious. Tom was not involved in everything, but often his name was just used to keep me in check.

# Chapter 21
# Lost Soul

Another time I told Tom that I felt like a lost soul. He answered, "Well, if that is how you feel, then I guess you are a lost soul, right?" That is after I was installed as queen witch. By that time I think they were preparing me for the fact that my soul *was* lost and were trying to get me used to that idea very slowly! That is how far they will go to show you how much you are under their control! I was so happy that he apparently cared so much about me!

I was so much under their control that in reality there was hardly anything left of my old self without me even realizing how much I had changed! Of course, I took it that it was out of Tom's love for me that all these things were happening to me, while in reality it was just another way to change me into the person the devil wanted me to become! And I felt so proud of it, because the devil made me think that it was out of Tom's sheer love for me that these things were done.

Another time I was in Holland for a family reunion, and we had rented a castle somewhere in Brabant, a province in Holland. At that time I was still smoking, and I wanted to go outside to smoke. I went to the hall to get my cigarettes out of my coat pocket, when I saw an apparition of about five people in the hallway, further down the hall, all dressed in eleventh century clothing.

One was a petite girl with beautiful, long, naturally curled dark hair. She was dressed in the clothing of those days, and was probably in her early twenties. Her dress was long and done in burgundy and ivory colours. She had one of those pointed hats on her head. She was in the company of an older gentleman and had two women with her, which looked to me like ladies in waiting. There was also one other younger man, probably the older man's son.

They were laughing and talking and having a good time. You could tell that she was the center figure in this scene. She looked backward at me, looked straight in my face, gestured with her head, winked at me and gave me the notion that I should follow them.

I didn't do it, because this happened twice in exactly the same way when I went for a cigarette! Of course, they always say that those old castles have ghosts in them, but this is really true since they disappeared around the corner where the renovations were being done. Maybe they remembered the happy times and did not want the renovations to take place!

# Chapter 22
## "No Name Satan"

All these things happen when you get involved with Satan and witchcraft. I never thought anything of it, took it as par for the course, and mentioned it to a niece of mine who had already told me I was a witch. She said, "Well, what else did you expect?" Believe it or not, I still thought that I was a pretty good girl and that there was nothing wrong with what I did!

I also was led to a store in Markham, where the owner of the store told me he had been expecting me. I was just driven there and taken to where they wanted me to go. Thinking back, it is so unbelievable that I was that far under Satan's control and still thinking it was Tom.

You see, every time I mentioned Tom's name I got an answer, so that was so implanted in my brain that I didn't know any better and just went along with everything! But then again, it *was* Tom who would tell me later, when I saw him again, that he had heard I had met one of his friends!

Oh, I forgot to mention the name of the devil or Satan will never come up until Satan thinks you are good and ready, and he thinks he has got you enough under his power that it is safe to make the switch.

Until that time it is a hidden thing, That is why these good-looking guys are always in charge, and their names are always in use whether they want it or not. It is not their decision but Satan's. Satan runs the show, and he tells them what has to be done to keep the souls from changing back to God.

When Satan thought I was ready for the changeover, he let me very subtly know that Tom had no idea what I was doing. The way that was put into my mind was after one of the night sessions. I was driving on the road and there was a bad accident. This was about the time that Tom was picking up his wife from work. As I was driving along I was given the thought in my head to see if by telepathy I could let Tom know that there was an accident on the road and that there was a big line of cars. I wanted to tell him to take an alternate route.

Since I had tried that on numerous occasions when it did work, I thought nothing of it at first. I tried hard to let it get through to him, but a little while later I saw him in the line of cars, and he didn't even see me! That was the first inkling I had that nothing had anything to do with him at all.

The next day I saw him in a store that we both frequented. I told him that Brenda was getting married, and he said, "Who the hell cares about that?" He told me in no uncertain words to get lost and not bother him anymore. I was hurt beyond belief and was furious. I told him he was going to be very sorry to have used me all those years and that he was going to be very sorry for that!

This was before the night the devil revealed himself. The next day I ended up in church and finally back with God. I was called a "traitor" by a very good friend who had been used before by Satan to give me messages when necessary. Well, on Brenda's wedding day I felt I was neglected by everyone. It was the devil's doing. I fully realized that, and there was nothing I could do about that.

The devil intended to make me feel like an outcast, and he succeeded in doing just that! He can manipulate anybody!

It had never happened before, and it was not anybody's fault. It was just the devil showing what he was capable of. It had nothing to do with Brenda, because Brenda is a sweetheart, and we have a very unique relationship as mother and daughter.

After my conversion back to God I told Brenda some of the things I had gone through, and she was sorry for me. She has always been very appreciative for the little bit I have done for her.

My 65th birthday was almost totally neglected, but again it was just the devil's doing to show me how by going back to God I had no right to ever enjoy myself again. I have had several incidents with my car and one small accident. These are just done out of revenge, so they don't bother me too much anymore!

Still, even now, there are still times that I know Satan is around. I have to be very careful that I don't swear or curse or lose my temper. He can get easily control over me again. I have to be always on my toes, and if you think that is easy, you have got to be kidding!

With the least little bit of trouble I know he is right around me again, and I have to start praying like crazy to get him to go away again. The thing is that I can't get rid of him totally again because I was so totally in his grasp. He does not want to give up, but believe you me, he has lost, whether he wants to realize this or not. He does not give up, and he always tries for another chance to get me back in his power. Well, as for me, once was too much and more than enough!

# Chapter 23
# Satan's Power over Men

All these guys that Satan has his power over have charisma pouring from them. You would think that butter wouldn't melt in their mouths, but they come straight from Satan, make no mistake about it. I have met several of them, and I tell you they are lady killers, every one of them! The devil knows how to pick them!

How he gets them is, he probably catches them when they are at a very low point in their life, are out of a job, need money badly, probably married with one or two small children, and that is where the devil does his dirty work and tells them that they can have money, a job, a car, and lots of goodies as long as they will do as he tells them and stay with the program!

He can also get them when they are young and vulnerable, as I know from one case where he got his hands on a boy of about eleven or twelve. The boy came from a broken home, where the father did not even recognize him as his son at the time. The mother had remarried a guy who I am pretty sure was into Satanism. When she divorced him she could not control her son anymore, and her second ex-husband offered to take him into his home. The mother agreed to that, and from then on he was totally impossible.

He got into Satanism at this early age and is now a totally lost soul. I would not hesitate to say that he is almost as far into this as Tom is. He tried it on his mother, but that did not work. I know that she has not seen him or her grandchildren again! I will write this case in a later chapter so you will read and understand that this went on from a very early age. That is why this book is so important, so that we all recognize the danger our whole society is in!

And some of them will and do turn their backs on him, but he gets enough of them! One is already too many! The thing is, he keeps his promise! These guys all make money and have everything, as long as they stay with the program!

And Tom stayed with the program, to the extent that I have seen his eyes turn from blue to yellow to an almost red colour. That happened when he was really riled up about something or someone!

That is a very scary sight to see happening in front of your eyes. After that happened he called me in his office and was very nice to me. He sort of let me know that it was not actually me he was mad at, but someone else who had upset him. He was just livid at the time.

Thinking back on things, I think he was mad at me for being around him all the time, but then he was told by the devil that he better cooperate or else! So he made up to me and was nice again!

Once when I was being driven again, the car made a wrong turn. I ended up on a dirt road. I kept yelling for help, but nothing happened, so I finally yelled, "Tom! Tom! Tom!"

That was the panic button signal, and I got an instant reply to turn around. I was driven to the right road. Things like that sometimes happened.

But I was also driven somewhere and saw two deer standing in the middle of the road. They stayed there till I could take a picture of them. Then another car came from the other side, and they jumped out of the way.

The devil responded to Tom's name! That it why this charade is so very dangerous! Single women are of course ideal for this purpose. They are mostly looking for a partner or are divorced like I am. We in the most vulnerable position as far as sex is concerned!

And believe it or not, the devil can make you believe anything he wants to. Make no mistake about that!!

# Chapter 24
# Satanism in Families

When the fathers are into Satanism, the little ones are mostly drawn into it by the fathers, who take this as a course to see how far their powers go to manipulate the whole family.

I know of one family where the man told me he was a super warlock, so I told him I was the queen witch. His wife has nothing to do with it, but he beats her up so badly that I am afraid she will become blind one of these days. Of course, she denies it all, but he has already made a little witch out of his oldest daughter. She is only five years old and is in her turn already beating up on her little sister, with daddy's blessing, because she has to learn early how to handle people and situations. He things she has to learn early to know how to handle people and situations. She is already totally under his power, and he is doing a good job on her. Without the child's knowledge he has already ruined her for life!

It is the same with the second one, who will only grow up with the idea that being beaten up is a natural way of living. She will think that being hit is something you just have to grin and bear, because that is what she sees her father do to the mother and her sister does to her!

I don't know how he is handling his son. I didn't stick around for that round as well, but it will be the devil's delight family. They are a good advertisement for him! It is a horrible feeling to see a whole family in such a predicament and knowing there is nothing I can do about it except pray that he will get his sanity one of these days.

Here in Canada I know that they start also as young as they can catch them, and then call them ankle biters. We have to somehow educate our children and grandchildren how to recognize the symptoms. That is not easy, however, because there are so many different ways in which they can catch them. We have to start by educating the adults first and then go on from there.

The idea that these things just don't happen is an unrealistic dream, a pipe dream, in fact. We should all wake up to the fact that Satan is definitely around and is not going to go away just because we don't want to believe in him.

Jesus did not give the Apostles the power to drive out demons for nothing. If we think that this only happened in the old days, then we are sadly mistaken. The devil is rampant all over the place.

Everyone is scared of the devil, and Satan knows this and is laughing his head off! He is thriving on the fact that everything is falling right into his hands. He gets exactly the leeway he needs to do his dirty work. And believe you me, it is dirty work! For me it was a reality, so nobody can tell me these things don't happen. If anyone knows, it is me. *I do know they happen*!

Of course, since I still was thought to believe that it was Tom that all these feelings came from, I didn't know any better and never thought anything about these kind of things. He even came into my dreams sometimes, even after seeing me pretty well all day. That, of course, was all the devil's doing and had nothing to do with Tom, but it made me believe more than ever that he was really in love with me! By that time he probably hated the very sight of me!

Once I was having lunch with Tom and his wife, believe it or not, when he all of a sudden he leaned back in his chair and there in the middle of the restaurant his face changed into a goat's head! His wife turned to him and said, "Hon-eeyy," and right away he changed back to his normal features!

I was totally flabbergasted. I had no idea anybody could do something like that and change their features to that extent! Actually this was in answer to a book that I was reading at home about witches and covens. I had been wondering if Tom would be a goat head; well, there was the answer to my question!

I knew he had Parkinson's disease, but he brought that one on himself with so much fooling around with his facial muscles. Either that or the devil made him change his face the way he wanted him to look. Whatever the reason, I have never seen anything like that in my life. You can also imagine that if it was possible for someone to change their features like that, than it would be possible for them to go by unrecognized by others!

Once I saw him, and he did not want to acknowledge me, but the devil literally took his head and turned it toward me. It was done with such a jerking motion that I am surprised he didn't have a broken neck after that. There is no way he could have done this himself.

While I was in seventh heaven, Tom was probably down in the pits the whole time. I doubt very much if his wife liked having a woman who was not bad to look at and had loads of money hanging around her husband!

I went to lunch a couple of times with Tom and his wife. I guess he was trying to tell me to lay off; he was going to stay married to his wife and that was it. But the devil did not think so, and he kept me around him all the time!

Then one night session he made me say the word "separate," and I started crying. I was made to understand that this meant that being Tom's "wife" was over, and I had better get used to it.

Of course I denied it and rejected the whole idea, but the next day Tom and his wife were standing outside the mall.

He looked at me and said, "Smile and say separate."

"No, no, no!" I answered him.

He just looked at me and said, "Yes."

He walked toward his wife, who was talking to some people. That was the end of my "marriage" to Tom.

And believe me or not, during the night sessions the devil kept on making me believe that Tom was still in love with me and that everything was all right! I was kept on to believe this because I was already so brainwashed!

Nobody who has not been on this path can have the faintest inkling how dangerous it is to get sucked so far into evil! Even as I am sitting here and typing all these things I feel the devil inside of me in the same way. That is a fight I will probably have for the rest of my life. I have got an idea that God is letting this happen so I can warn other people how to react when they get into a similar situation! Don't ever think that it would never happen to you, that would be the first mistake you make. If it can happen to me, so can it happen to you. Be forewarned!

I never in my whole life thought I would ever be in this situation, but it is still where I ended up. I grew up very religious and thought myself as quite religious. As a matter of fact, when I was about fifteen years old I wanted to become a nun. My dad kind of talked me out of that. No father likes to see his daughter become a nun, of what I have heard!

But I really thought that I was quite a good Catholic, and I was a good Catholic until we went to Canada. Then after a while some things happened. I didn't get the answers to questions I had and slowly but surely I started to drift away from the church, which was a pity and should never have happened. I actually was Catholic, but in name only at the time. Without realizing it, the devil had already a good stronghold over me, and I didn't even recognize it!

They don't know what it is like to finally, after six years, get to know that you are going to make it to high priestess. You get the world offered on a silver platter, if you will only give in and worship the devil. The only thing the devil wants to hear you say is, "Satan. Satan."

You first have to renounce everything that is worthwhile. After all, he knows exactly what you need, and you will get it if you only renounce God and worship Satan. He will give you the world on a silver platter (and forget about that too, because there are more lies in that statement than you can think up in a lifetime!).

You have to do exactly as he dictates, and even then you get "punished" for any little thing that you do wrong. Also, there are things that will happen to your health and body that you won't like, but he's got you by then, or so you believe. One example is that I like swimming and used to go for my daily swim. Sometimes, whenever Satan felt like it, he would make me lose my breath under water, or I would choke and would just about drown. That was just to show me how dependent I was on his wiles!

*But never forget that God is there also, and He will take you back in a flash. Just because you have a free will, and God will let you do what you want, does not mean He will leave you alone. He will take you back if you ask Him!*

The devil will tell you that you had better give in to Satan, because he has you hanging in midair sexwise. That feeling does not go away, it is very persistent. He makes you feel so high, and you are totally helpless. That is a very lousy feeling, I can tell you! And he keeps you there till you finally say, "Oh yes, oh yes!" because you need the relief so bad!

And then there was this thing he made me do that is kind of hard to explain, but I'll try. He made my hands go down the length of my body, all the way to my feet. It seemed like I picked up something from the bottom of my feet, the way you would take off a long gown. I brought it up over my head to discard it on the floor, then my hands were brought to the bottom of my feet and would go up the whole length of my body, with the definite feeling that I was being put in a bag or a sack. When my hands were on top of my head, he twisted my fingers round and round as if I was tying up the bag. I had the distinct feeling that after that was done, I heard him say, "That one's in the bag!"

When that happened I really felt I was choking quite literally! That is the time when I said, "I am choking. I have to get out of this. I have to talk to a priest, I need to get exorcised!"

I had been going to church with a friend of mine and was arrogant enough to even go to communion, because the devil will tell you that it is quite all right to do so! After all, you haven't killed anybody, and you are quite a good Catholic, so you can easily do your thing. He will let you do that, because in his eyes you are already his. It mocks God, so this made it even worse for me. I went ahead and thought nothing of it!

# Chapter 25
# My Conversion

But this time I started by asking God for help, and I received it immediately. He must have been waiting for it! The next morning I got a phone call from a friend in the building, asking me if I wanted to go to church with her. I said yes and went with her, but I felt all choked up in church. Then I thought, I have to do something more than this! I have to work it differently, I have to talk to a priest and get exorcized.

For one or another reason I got the message in my head that I had to go to St. Therese de la Petite Fleur church. I was too afraid to listen to any messages, though, in fear that they were concocted by the devil. I was too scared to listen to this ever-so-clear message.

I went to a church which was closed, of course, because it had not penetrated my brain yet that I had to go to St. Therese church. I wasn't thinking of the fact that the devil was trying very hard to keep me from going there, so was trying very hard to implant the message that I would not be getting anywhere. But I persisted, and I did end up at St. Therese church. The door opened up and miraculously the priest there had just gotten a cancellation. He had some free time for me. Well, we talked for two and a half hours.

He gave me this time, which I really needed, because I started pouring out my heart. I was crying, told him all the things that had happened, and then I asked for forgiveness and absolution. I asked if I could please, please, please be exorcized. I started praying with him. I did my confession then and there, and after that I went to another church for the first Mass that was of benefit to me after a long time!

Oh, I felt I was walking on clouds after that! I felt such an enormous relief during that time that I felt reborn and that God was so good to me to show me His infinite love. But God knows better and just made sure I ended up there!

Father Bill gave me two and a half hours of his time, and I have never in my whole life been so grateful to anybody for this oh-so-precious time given to cleanse myself. He told me I would have to pray for the rest of my life to be free of Satan and to be very diligent and on my toes to keep him away from me.

The next day I was told by one of my best friends, "You are a traitor." Since I knew what she meant by that, I asked her why she was saying this, and she said, "I don't know why I am saying this, but I have to say that you are a traitor." Of course, it was perfectly clear to me why she said it. She had been used by Satan before to give me a message about something, so I wasn't surprised at that, but it just shows how powerful he is and that he can use anybody or anything, and that includes my cats.

Right now I am getting very bad vibes from Donner, my black cat. He is constantly around me and is being made to do things to break my concentration.

I had not been to church for a while and had really slowed down my religious efforts. I still thought myself as Catholic! Incredible! I have a lot to make up for, and I am working on it and am atoning for what has happened in the past on a daily basis. That is why writing this book is so important to me, because it is meant as a warning to everybody to *please, please, please* be aware of what is happening in the world and all the evil that daily surrounds us. Stay close to God and know deep within your heart that His love for us is *bottomless*.

God just pours out His infinite love and compassion and graces on us; we only have to ask for them and will receive them in abundance! When I first started going back to church and had my first confession with Father Bill, I had all sorts of poltergeists in my place. Everything was clanging and banging. The toilets, both of them at the same time, would get backed up or the handles would break and both had to be replaced. Often something would break that had no business breaking! I heard and felt things I had never had any problem with. I got holy water and sprinkled it all around and on the cats.

I went on a pilgrimage to Nebraska that was set up by the brothers and sisters of the Alliance of the Two Hearts. It was so incredibly beautiful, and I was so full of adoration for the Two Hearts. It was so powerful. There were about four or five hundred teenagers. The whole four days were inundated with religion, prayers, rosaries and processions. It was amazing.

It was there that my adoration for the Two Sacred Hearts of Jesus and Mama Maria started, and it has only increased since then!

We had a beautiful High Mass with the Archbishop and two other priests. One was Father John and one was Father Bing, but I can't remember the other ones. The devotion to the Two Hearts is so enormous there, and the Holy Spirit is everywhere. We could just feel Him in the air all around us!

I thought I had cried a lot with Father Bill, but here it went on continuously and nobody minded. Everyone was crying and laughing, praying, hugging and filled with love for everyone.

The processions were so incredible. We would start at the church and then in procession, carrying the big statue of Our Lord Jesus in front and a large statue of Mama Maria, we would either pray the rosary or sing Mama Maria's songs along the way. The people would come out of their houses and either join us in the procession or stand by the door and join us in praying. They would kneel down for Our Lord Jesus or for Mama Maria, but there was not one that ignored us or made a rude comment!

I was talking to a priest there and told him of my story, but he told me I had nothing to be afraid of anymore. He told me he could see that the devil had no more power over me, and told me to keep on praying and focus my life on God and my faith and I would be all right!

He also told me that I would have to pray for the rest of my life, more so than others, to keep Satan away from me! That made me feel better, as he is an exorcist. He knew what he was talking about! It seems that wherever I turned I was getting encouragement!

They were also selling a lot of rosaries and stuff, so I picked up a whole bunch of rosaries and hung them all over my condo. I got statues and planted them all around and got everything blessed in sight!

I got hold of the intergenerational prayer and will say that every once in a while, whenever necessary. While I am working on my book right now, I heard from my youngest son that my granddaughter broke her arm tonight. That also is the devil at work! The poor little thing, she is only eight years old, but Satan is pretty angry right now and took it out not on me. But he did indirectly, oh yes! So I am going to say that prayer right away!

All in all I did everything that was possible to get rid of the devil, poltergeists and any such things that I was afraid of hanging in and around my place. I prayed like crazy, and every time something went wrong I prayed to St. Michael, which I still do. Things have slowed down to an enormous extent!

Never forget that the devil will use your friends or relatives, literally anybody to thwart you if you want to do good. If at any time you get a message or a comment that would make you angry, think that it is the devil doing his thing and stay clear of it! Lots of people are being used to create fights, arguments, murders and hurting other people just so the devil can do his thing. If we all are aware and are cognizant of this, we can create a better world!

Thanks be to God! I have to give thanks to the whole court of heaven. I think I have asked just about everyone for help! Mama Maria has been amazing to me. I have received so many graces and help from her. She is really my mother!

As always, but especially now, the priests have been under the attack of the devil, especially the charismatic priests. It is happening very subtly, and they don't even have the faintest idea that this is what is happening.

For all the priests who have helped and encouraged me, but also for all the priests the whole world over, I am going to write this following prayer. You need our help and support:

## A Prayer for Priests

*Keep them, I pray Thee, dearest Lord. Keep them, for they are Thine*
*The priests whose lives burn out before Thy consecrated shrine*
*Keep them, for they are in the world, though from the world apart*
*When earthly pleasures tempt—allure—shelter them in Thy heart.*
*Keep them and comfort them in hours of loneliness and pain*
*When all their life of sacrifice for souls seems but in vain.*
*Keep them and, oh, remember, Lord, they have no one but Thee*
*Yet they have only human hearts, with human frailty.*
*Keep them as spotless as the Host that daily they caress*
*Their every thought and word and deed*
*Deign, dearest Lord, to bless.*
*Our Father, etc. Hail Mary, etc.*
*Queen of the clergy, pray for them.*

The Holy Spirit is unbelievable. He is constantly in and on my mind. The Holy Trinity is awesome! Oh, the help you receive when you just ask God for help is so totally amazing!

Before I started to go back to church I started to get bad pain in my left hip, in my fingers, and in my lower back. I thought and was told that arthritis was setting in. After all, I was 64 years old, so that could happen, right?

Well, since I have gone back to God and the church I went on a pilgrimage to Quebec and got a bottle of the oil at St. Joseph's Oratory, which has healing power. It is powerful and it works like a charm. My hip is totally okay now; my fingers are almost all right; my nails have grown back to normal and are actually growing, they don't break off anymore; I have no more pain in my toes; all my aches and pains are gone; and I haven't even taken an aspirin for the pain. I feel terrific! Isn't God wonderful?

We went on a retreat to Merlyn, Ontario, with a group of nine buses. Before we left from Toronto, it was raining. We heard that it was going to rain all day, from the pessimists, but I kept on saying the sun was going to shine for us in Merlyn and to stop yapping about rain. Since I think most of us were praying for the same thing, we did have sunshine the closer we got to Merlyn, which is only three hours away from Toronto. We did have sunshine the whole day. So someone asked me how I knew, and I told her that if you believe in something, it will happen.

People forget the faith thing very easily, but each time I have total faith, especially in Mama Maria. What I ask for will happen, because I thank for it at the same time, and it is granted already. And that is what faith is all about!

I still feel I have to get rid of my cats, because I think Donner is a channel for the devil and he is easily used as such. In the beginning when I had returned to God and the church I was praying in front of the Holy Mary statue, when he was quite literally thrown on my back. I had some bad scratches, but this happened a couple of times. Once when I was praying in bed he was also thrown on top of me. I had been having some stomach trouble, so you can imagine how that felt!

He can come and be with me and then somehow or other bites or nibbles at my fingernails, and they will either break or get chipped when I wear nail polish. He will jump on my shoulder and nibble on my hair, then it might fall flat or I will loose the curl. I have made inquiries to have the cats adopted, and it is as if they know something is up.

Donner is very quiet and stays out my way, which is very unusual for him. He just sits at the entrance to the computer room. Blitzen is her usual self, but also very subdued! Donner is right now too good to be true, and I think he is being kept quiet on purpose, so now I definitely know he has to go!

It used to be a lot worse than it is now, but I still have moments that I think he is still under the influence of the devil, and I still have to watch out, especially when I want to work on this book. I feel the devil's presence sometimes, but it does not scare me the way it used to. I am more confident of myself now and know I can always tap into the Holy Spirit. He will come down in a hurry to stand by me!

Now when I am typing away and I get that feeling inside of me, I tap into the Holy Spirit in a hurry and pray to St. Michael that it will go away again. It is not only I that thinks the cats have to go. I have a very good friend that says the same thing, and since she is very devout and holy and has been slain and anointed by the Holy Spirit, the same as I have been, I believe her absolutely!

Sometimes she reads what I have written down and it gives her the shivers on her back, but I have lived through this hell and am writing this only to help other people so they will be able to recognize the scenario and stay clear of this. Believe me, it is not worth your while to get yourself ensnared in this!

If anyone thinks it is fun to bring all these painful memories back or to get that feeling back again, then they are sadly mistaken. I want to be rid of them! But unless I finish this book I don't think I will have the ghost of a chance to be free of it! This is what I was meant to do, and I had better finish it in a hurry!

It is almost like a final cleansing of my soul, and I have to do this in order to be totally free of everything and to let the devil know I am God's child for always.

I ask St. Michael to come to my assistance whenever I feel threatened and then I am allright again.

Nobody can imagine, how the devil works.

People think they know, but when I hear them talk, I think to myself, You have no idea what you are talking about! You don't know anything!" And people really don't know!

People who *should* know do *not* want to listen to the ones who have been there and have come out of it by God's grace and help. They don't want to listen to those of us that had the guts to renounce the devil and ask God for forgiveness and hope and trust and know they will receive it! They don't know how the devil gets his way around them, because they all think they are in control of everything and they know exactly what they are doing! Oh boy, can they be wrong!

The devil loves anyone who thinks they have the world by the tail, because these people are the most vulnerable as far as Satan is concerned. He already has them halfway in his back pocket. All they need is a little shove, and they are his for the taking! He has his way with anyone who is not constantly on his or her toes to make sure these things do not happen to them!

*All of mankind has to realize that without God we can't even take a breath. Without Jesus' crucifixion we would not exist; without the power of the Holy Spirit we would all be lost souls!*

Even now I am constantly tempted by Satan while I am writing this, and I have to keep the image of God constantly in front of my eyes and ask St. Michael to stand by me and the Holy Spirit to stay by me and ask my Mama Maria to help and guide me!

Now it is getting closer to full moon, of course, the attacks are worse than normal. But finally last night after a session of crying the blues to Jesus that things weren't getting any better, I got the message to hang crosses of any size in the windows facing the moon. After that I prayed the intergenerational prayer with the picture of the Sacred Heart of Jesus in front of me. I had instant relief. It was as if the whole place was instantly cleansed!

No, you can't get rid of it without exorcism, but you can control it by praying and dedicating your life to God and letting Jesus be your guide in everything. Always stay close to the Holy Spirit, who is your source of love. That is one thing that the devil hates, and then you know that you are safe. Make sure that you get slain by the Holy Spirit when you are ready for this, and you will be with God always.

I am a child of Jesus. I am totally in His care; I have dedicated my life to Him and Mama Maria, and the Holy Spirit has control over the rest of me! And God the Father looks over all of this and smiles!

Even now that feeling is back inside of me to remind me how close the devil is, and he is letting me know that he is not far away from me still, even now that I have gone back to God and the church! I think I was put through this so I can tell my story so other people will learn from it and will take better heed than I did and not be as gullible as I was!

Another way to get rid of the devil is to offer everything up to God to praise Him, to glorify Him, to honor Him, and to let Him use all the things that are happening to you for the greater glory of God. He can use these things according to His holy will! You have no idea how fast you can get rid of anything that is wrong at that moment as long as it was invented by the devil to oppose your turning to God.

You will be made to feel like a pariah by some people when you tell your story or part of it. They don't know what it is like and subsequently have no idea how to react to you anymore.

Or you may have a spiritual warfare going on, and then the devil decides that it would be a good idea to turn your friends against you. And don't think this does not happen—it has happened to me numerous times! That is when I ask Jesus to hide me in His holy wounds and ask Mama Maria to hold me, because it seems at that time that everyone has turned against me. I would feel so lonely and desolate, yet I couldn't tell these friends because they would not and do not understand it. Not that they are dummies, but they have absolutely no idea what I was going through and how the devil could change their thinking!

It hurts to see people you really like and honor their friendship seem to turn against you when there is nothing you can do about it! Things will turn around again once you start praying and ask God to please turn the people back to you. Wait till it happens—it happens pretty fast!

I have talked to somebody who is going through the same experience I am going through, and I am amazed how similar the devil is in his wiles and ways. He seems to have a one-track mind. We have both gone through pretty well the same things!

The more these things happen, of course, the more of an idea I get. I definitely have to write this book and to keep on going with it. It is more an incentive than they figured on, I guess.

You know, it finally dawned on me that actually I had not been happy all that time, and the peace that I had always felt before I got into this is finally back with me now. I am much calmer, I don't smoke or drink or swear anymore. All that has disappeared from my life; I don't miss it at all, and I feel so close to God, Jesus the Holy Spirit and Mama Maria. There are no words to describe how different I feel now that it is all over!

I was talking to a woman in the store this afternoon who told me that in all the seven or eight years she has known me, I have never looked so peaceful and serene. I thought, THANK YOU, GOD! It was the best compliment I could have gotten from anybody!

Yesterday I had the same thing happen with my car quitting on me twice in a row, but today I had no problem with it!

I was watching the stations of the cross tonight and had to cry for all the pain and sorrow I had caused by my selfish behaviour, not realizing how much my Lord Jesus had suffered for my sins. I felt so bad that I had to ask forgiveness again for all the things that had happened and to promise again that I have dedicated my life to my Lord Jesus. The love I now have in my heart for Jesus is formidable, and I hope it continues to grow with time and prayers.

I also have asked the Holy Spirit to please keep me humble and let me not forget and grow complacent again.

I have dedicated my life to the Lord, and He is making me do all sorts of good things. This includes writing this book now, and believe you me, this is not an easy task. The devil thinks he has a way in again and is trying very hard again to win me back. I don't think he will succeed!

Under the divine guidance of God, my Saviour, I saw a small white icon one night after I went back to God. It was Jesus, who said, "Maria, I want you to do things *My* way from now on."

All I could say was, "Yes, my Lord."

The next morning after Holy Mass I was having coffee, and I picked up a cigarette. I heard an inner voice very distinctly say, "You don't need this anymore!"

"Yes, my Lord."

I put the cigarette down and quit smoking just like that, and I have never missed it for a second. I feel a lot better for it! After 44 years I don't even miss it!

Before I quit, my doctor had been telling me to please quit smoking, that I was doing irreparable damage to my lungs. So after I quit I had to go and see him for my yearly check-up. He sent me to a specialist, saying now he was going to show me the damage I had done with all my smoking. I got so scared and started thinking of cancer!

Well, the specialist said the same thing, so I went for x-rays. When the results were in I went back to the specialist, and he kind of looked funny at me and said, "How long did you smoke for?"

"For 44 years," I told him.

And he said, "But you did not smoke much."

I told him that I started when I was seventeen by just one or two cigarettes, but that after I came to Canada it increased steadily to about one pack per day. I came to Canada in 1960.

He just couldn't believe it, the x-rays showed up perfectly clear. There was nothing there, so this was incredible! He told me that never in his entire practice had he seen this happening, so I said to him that it was divine intervention and that God gave graces when you returned to Him.

He sent the x-rays to my doctor, who also looked at me funny and said he could not believe it either. I told him too that it must have been a very divine intervention, because I had gone back to God and it was He who told me to quit smoking! Ever since then he asks me if I want a prescription, but most of the time I tell him it is not necessary! And they *aren't* necessary!

Jesus is the divine healer, and anyone can ask Him for healing. People just do not think the right way!

I went to Marmora, Ontario, with Betty, friend of mine, on a day's pilgrimage. It was her first trip to Marmora. This is a place where Mama Maria often gives signs and appears quite often.

As we arrived around eleven-thirty in the morning, and I was waiting for my friend outside the washroom area, I saw a streak of pink in the sky and thought, That is funny. I closed my eyes and shook my head. I opened my eyes, and by this time Betty had joined me and the colours had intensified. There were a myriad of beautiful colours in the sky and also a small white cloud in the air in the shape of a white dove. The white dove is the sign of the Holy Spirit.

Even though the clouds were moving, the colours and the white dove cloud stayed put and didn't move. We were very moved by this, but continued and did all the stations of the cross and prayed the rosary.

At around four o'clock, as we were having a bite to eat, a lady came to us and introduced herself as Lorraine. She sat with us and told us that she was from Sudbury, Ontario, which is a fair distance away, about a seven or eight hour drive. She had been organizing these pilgrimages for years, and it was her twenty-third pilgrimage. She said could not do them anymore. She didn't look that old to us, but she was close to eighty years old. She could have easily passed for sixty!

She told us that she had asked Mama Maria to give her a sign as a thank you for all the years and efforts she had put in, but the bus was late arriving, so she had totally missed the noon signs. I said, "Why don't we ask Mama Maria for a sign now?"

They both said that it was ridiculous to just ask for something, but I said very simply, "Mama Maria, Lorraine from Sudbury would like a sign from you as a thank you for all the time and effort she has put into all these pilgrimages. She missed the noon signs. Can you please give her a sign? Thank you for listening to us."

After this very short prayer I told them to look up in the sky, but they were looking at me as if I had lost my marbles. I told them to look up in the sky and not at me, and the sun started to spin around with a beautiful dark blue disk in front. If the blue disk would not be there we could have gone blind looking straight in the sun. As soon as the disk was there it was safe to look at the sun. The aura around the sun was beautiful as it was spinning counterclockwise. The colours were changing all the time, and then after about five minutes there appeared a beautiful gold cross! It was a totally incredible sight, and we thanked Mama Maria for it. Lorraine was so happy!

Everyone was laughing, crying and hugging each other and taking pictures of this miracle. We were all so totally in awe by this beautiful sight! Oh, it was incredible and so very, very special. It goes to show that when you firmly believe in something, it is going to happen. I had never a doubt that Mama Maria would give a sign, but *with childlike trust* had no doubt in my mind that it would happen!

I am not telling you this story to glorify myself, but rather to show you that if you have enough faith you can move mountains. In this case I was the vessel that was used to show that through a real show of faith things will happen! All these stories are not being told for sensationalism, but to show you with faith anything is possible!

Another time Betty and I went to a restaurant for lunch, and she knew one of the waiters there. He came over and asked her if she would pray over him, so we joined hands and then prayed over him. A couple of the other waiters came over, and we did the same for them. The night before we had been to a healing Mass and were slain by the Holy Spirit. Betty was used as a tool to help these people, and I was just tagging along with her!

The next week I was talking to a lady I know, and I asked her how she was doing since I knew she had cancer of the liver. I promised to pray for her and her family, but after I talked to her and hung up the phone, Betty said that we could pray *over* her as well, so I phoned her back and asked her if that is what she would like us to do. So we went there and prayed over her and the cancer went into remission and was shrinking when she went back to the hospital for a check-up and chemotherapy! With faith, God's help and Jesus' healing hands you can move mountains!

# Chapter 26
# St. Therese of the Little Flower

This episode is about St. Therese de Lisieux, who is a very powerful saint. She helps people to convert back to church. I say a couple of prayers to her every day for different intentions. One day Betty and I came back from church, and we were going for breakfast to my place.

We got out of my car, and as we entered the building there was a guy standing there with a bouquet of pink roses in his hands, which is a sign of St. Therese.

I looked at him and said, "Beautiful roses."

And he said, "Yes, beautiful roses for a beautiful lady."

He held out his arms to me, but I never thought that anyone would ever give me roses, so I said that she was a very lucky lady. I thought, Thank you, St. Therese. This is a sign I needed to see that you are helping me. I never thought that this was an angel sent by her to me with the roses, because they *were* meant for me!

We went to the ground floor to pick up my mail. The angels left the elevator with us and stood to the side of the elevators without the roses. I heard a long time later that since I did not accept the roses, my guardian angel accepted them in my name.

I heard Betty talking behind me, but thought she was talking to the lady who I could see out of the corner of my eye and who also went in the elevator with us. But now, come to think of it, I think she was also an angel, because Betty said she was talking to me the whole time and there was nobody but the two of us. This lady, whoever it was, was smiling but did not say anything. I never really had a clear view of her; she was sort of in the background.

I did not take the roses from him, because I could not believe that anybody would give me pink roses. I let him get away from me, because angels are very shy and don't impose themselves on anybody! This is such a beautiful story and absolutely true! Since then I have seen signs that St. Therese is hard at work for me!

On November 19, Father John Paul Villanueva from a Parish in Mississauga invited me to go to Kitchener. My friend Betty went with us. He was going to be the celebrant in the Holy Mass, and a very powerful visionary from Florida, by the name of Flor Maria del Rosario Achong, was going to be there. I felt so privileged.

He wanted me to meet her and talk to her. Seldom have I met anybody so humble and in God's hands as this lady! She laid on hands, she was inundated with the Holy Spirit, and you could feel the presence of God wherever she was. It was amazing. I felt so blessed when she laid her hands on me, and I was slain by the Holy Spirit.

Her story is an amazing one.

Her mother died at her birth and left her as an orphan. Since she was crippled, nobody really wanted her. She grew up on the streets in Florida and in orphanages. She was, however, a very happy child. She always had a smile for everyone she encountered, though they were never returned. Because of malnutrition she was blind and had terrible sores and boils all over. This created pus. She had scars all over her body, and people would literally go out of their way to avoid her.

Even with all the misfortunes she had to deal with, she was still always happy with an inner happiness that was her very own. She was, through her love for everyone and everything, so well protected by God. That must have been a built-in knowledge, because whenever she encountered a picture of Jesus she would say "Tata" and smile.

Later, through being in an orphanage around nuns, she got to know God, Jesus, the Holy Spirit and, of course, Mama Maria.

Whenever she saw a picture of Jesus she would say, "Tata."

It also came to the surface that she was actually visited by Jesus and Mama Maria. She frequently talked to them, but that came out later on.

Since she was so ugly, whenever she was in an orphanage and it was adoption time she was always pushed to the side. She was not a good prospect for adoption. But one time they were a little late with the pushing out of the way. There was a lady who saw her and asked for her name.

She told her, "My name is Flor Maria del Rosario."

This lady, who was very Marian, decided to adopt her; she loved her name.

Since she never had a birth certificate, she is not sure of her exact age, but is between 53 and 56. She looks around 40! Now people come flocking to her and can't leave her alone! She is beautiful inside and outside! Isn't it amazing the way God's plans work out?

Father John Paul is a true lover of the Blessed Mother and of the Holy Eucharist, and he sometimes sends me e-mails with the most amazing messages that make my whole day beautiful. I end up loving God and the Holy Trinity and Mama Maria more than ever!

He is a true inspiration to the priesthood, has got the Holy Spirit in his backpocket, and he takes Him out whenever possible to share Him with us. We all get slain with the Holy Spirit, are all full of love and are all the better for it!

I was asked to give my testimony in the church with a few hundred people there! I had no idea I was supposed to do that, so I was not prepared at all. I asked the Holy Spirit to please guide me, and I did give my testimony. It was more a declaration of faith and about my return to God then a message to people to stay out of the hands of Satan! But I guess God wanted it that way. After all, it was His doing that I was there at all. All praise, glory and honor should go to Him!

The spiritual warfare I have gone through this time was a very heavy one. I always think that I must have been doing some things right to make the devil so angry that he would retaliate! In the prayer group I am in we had a session called "The Life of the Spirit." I missed most of those because I got sick with pneumonia, laryngitis, sinusitis and consequently a middle-ear infection. You can see I went the whole gambit! Needless to say, I missed most of those sessions.

I had the trip to Kitchener coming up, and I was afraid that I was going to miss it too, but I prayed to Jesus, who is after all the Healer in this world. I got better and did go! Not everything went smooth there, though. After all, the devil had to have a little say in it too!

We went there and got safely back again, which Jesus had promised me, so all was well. I had a lot of dizzy spells that whole day for no reason that I could see. You can see that you can have interference on every level!

If we will only keep an open mind about things and realize that God tries us in His own way, we have also to come to the conclusion that He will put us to the test at any time. I think He will do this especially around Christmastime, because some of the beggars you meet are really angels sent to earth to see if we can give as easy as we take.

I have once seen such an angel at an outside mall. I gave him some money, and he blessed me! I looked at him, and I have seldom seen such an honest and open face! When I went back to give him some more change from the car, he was gone! I asked somebody at a stand that he had been sitting next to where he was, but the guy told me that he never saw anybody sitting there!

What we have to keep in mind is to show at all times total trust in God and in His goodness and love for us, that we will and do receive the things we ask for, as long as we leave the decision up to Him and trust in His ultimate plan for us and do not question His decision!

*God is so good to me, He gives me everything I need!*

# Chapter 27
# The Cats Have to Go

I did get rid of the cats. I took them to the Humane Society, because of Donner. I did not care to take the chance that somebody else would get a cat that was possessed, so I brought them there on a Tuesday.

A couple of nights later I woke up, and as I am want to do, I was praying a chaplet. In the middle of praying I heard meowing and saw the image of Blitzen on her hind paws, putting her front paws in the air the way she used to when she wanted to be picked up. Then the meowing stopped, and she was gone. I have an idea she was euthanized at that time. I am sorry for what I felt I absolutely had to do, for she was a beautiful little cat. I really loved her.

I have been given a lot to offset the loss of my cats and am busy with church work, the R.C.I.A. and the C.W.L. I teach the rosary in several places, I belong to the Legion of Mary, a prayer group, the Sacristy work, Eucharistic ministry, and the lectors once a week. So as you can see I am being kept very busy.

I have recently met a nice girl who, at the age of 34, still a virgin. She is a very devout Catholic and as such she is a target that the devil just cannot leave alone.

MARWEN

She lives in the most evil surroundings that, when I gave her a ride home after a healing Mass, as soon as we entered the driveway, the hair on my back was standing up straight. I have only once more in my life felt so much evil surrounding me! I told her that in no way was I going to stay and have a chat in the car with her. I turned the car around and looked for a church in order to get rid of the evil around us. We drove around and talked for a while, and then I dropped her off at her apartment building and went home.

The next day as I went out of the parking lot and onto the street, an enormous spider came right in front of my face, hanging inside the car. I just screamed and screamed till I got to the church. Apparently I drove like a maniac and passed several people who were also going to Mass. They asked me what was wrong when I got to church. Somebody took me to a store, we bought insect repellent, sprayed about half the can in there, and then we went to Mass.

I know that it was done to scare me, but I also could have had a very bad car accident. I also know that Satan doesn't like to lose a soul, and he sure has lost me!

Without her being aware of the fact, the devil interferes more in this woman's life than she realizes. That is something I am trying to get her to realize!

It is also something she does not want to believe, because she figures since her home is blessed she is okay and nothing can attack her. She thinks that Satan has no hold over her, but I know very well there are ways and means to get through to her. He is trying very hard to accomplish this!

I was talking to her this morning and asked her permission to use her story for my book, which she gave me, praise the Lord. We were talking for a while. Her situation is getting better lately, and I hope for her sake this keeps up!

I have finally come to the conclusion that since she is using too many intergenerational prayers she is provoking and invoking the devil, and this is not doing herself any good.

That is something we have to be very careful with. I sometimes say an intergenerational prayer when it is really needed, but the powerful prayers you should only say when they are really needed.

Regular prayers are all right to say, but with intergenerational prayers you have to be very discerning, because you can actually provoke and invoke the devil to come and do his stuff instead of turning him away from you and your family. You can actually do more harm than good in some cases.

You also have to be very careful with your friends and family with these kind of prayers, because you can also invoke him on your family as well!

If anyone thinks it is an easy task that after you have been involved with Satanism all you have to do is go back to God and all will be well, you are sadly mistaken. The devil is on your neck, and make no mistake about it, he is there to stay. It is constantly up to you through prayers and constant vigil that you will stay with God, because the devil will try in every way, shape or form to get to you!

Even now I have to constantly think how he works! Always ask the Holy Spirit for discernment. You will know what the devil is up to, and you will get your answers. You will not be left alone. The help is always there, just dig in to the resources open to you.

The prayer group I am in has a "Life in the Spirit" session that is eight weeks long. I was really looking forward to this, because I love the Holy Spirit, but I have only been able to attend three sessions so far. I got sick and was out of commission for four weeks, and I have missed four sessions in total, but I am going to do it again some time in the future.

At the moment he is trying to keep me away from the Holy Spirit and anything that has to do with that. So, again, through the inspiration of the Holy Spirit, I had the discernment to realize what was happening. I can fight him now on his own grounds and not let him interfere anymore with this part of my life. The closer I get to God, the more harm he is trying to do to me!

But don't be discouraged, he won't win! And that is the attitude each one of us should have when we are in the same situation. He cannot win if you don't let him, and also don't forget that Jesus does not lose out to Satan. He is not going to lose you again to the devil, so you stay close to God and you'll be fine! He will cradle you in His arms like a baby and will love you like the lost sheep that has been found!

People do not realize how much evil there is around us all. They think you are crazy to talk about these things, but if you have personally experienced this, you know that it is far worse than people realize. We really need to pray to God for deliverance from this in our lives. Our very breath we owe to the goodness of God, but not enough of us are willing to give Him credit for His creation.

*All God wants from us is acknowledgment of His greatness and His love for us.*

I don't think that is too much to ask of the sacred heart of Jesus, do you?

# Chapter 28
# The Goodness of God

We had a beautiful Easter vigil in the church. We had five candidates in the R.C.I.A., four of which were baptized with the Holy Eucharist. One was the twenty-month-old son of Ann, who was being baptized together with her son. To everyone's amazement, her little one never even cried when the water was poured over his head.

My candidate had her first reconciliation, her confirmation and her first communion. She was already baptized before. The other two were a mother and her twelve-year-old daughter, who were also baptized, had their confirmation and their first communion.

It was a beautiful ceremony, and the whole church was asked to participate in it. They got a good applause as a welcome to the church, and it was quite emotional with all the handshakes and hugs that went on afterward. Of course there were lots of pictures taken, and we had a reception for them after Mass, which was quite nice. There was an exchange of gifts and congratulations, and there was a nice cake with their names on it. It was a very rewarding experience and one that I would like to have again!

I have also had the vision of the Sacred Heart of Jesus with the thorns all around the heart. Where the wound is from the lance there was a monstrance with the Holy Eucharist coming out of it.

I had a vision of Jesus and Mama Maria as appears on the picture of the Divine Mercy Chaplet, and on the ground in front of Him was Satan writhing. He said to Jesus, "That is not fair! If that keeps up I won't have any left!"

Jesus answered Him, "Go away, Satan!"

Then he disappeared. Jesus was still standing there, then the whole scene faded away.

My life is full of God's love, which totally and completely envelops me and is now so very rewarding. That is the way God wants it for me, and that is the way I want it to be for the rest of my life!

I have the everlasting love and joy of God in my heart, and I will never want to see this changed!

There is a beautiful litany of humility which I pray now all the time. Believe you me, I need it badly! It will make anybody humble just by reading it and by applying it. The litany becomes a source of power and strength! I think that the good Lord is using me as a tool to get through to people who need help, and that is as it should be.

I have totally dedicated myself to the Holy Trinity and the alliance of the two hearts of Jesus and Mary. God is good, all the time!

And there just is no room for anything else in my life!

Isn't life just absolutely marvelous? If you just let God have His way with you, then all you have to do is say, "Yes, my Lord."